LORD of the SEA
Shark and Man

Sunlight reflecting through water gives a hammerhead shark uncharacteristic stripes. While the function of its oddly shaped head is not fully understood, the hammerhead is one of the only five or six species, out of 250 or more, known occasionally to attack man. (Doug Wallin/Taurus Photos)

Shark and Man

By the Editors of COUNTRY BEAUTIFUL
Publisher and Editorial Director: Michael P. Dineen
Executive Editor: Robert L. Polley
Text by Joseph John

COUNTRY BEAUTIFUL
Waukesha, Wisconsin

COUNTRY BEAUTIFUL: *Publisher and Editorial Director:* Michael P. Dineen; *Vice President, Editorial:* Robert L. Polley; *Vice President, Operations:* Donna Griesemer; *Managing Editor:* John M. Nuhn; *Art Director:* Buford Nixon; *Senior Editors:* James H. Robb, Kenneth L. Schmitz, Stewart L. Udall; *Associate Editors:* Kay Kundinger, Wendy Weirauch (House Editor); *Editorial Assistant:* Julie Fischer; *Art Assistant:* Ann Baer; *Production & Sales:* Mary Moran; *Marketing:* John Dineen; *Assistant to Publisher:* Gay Ciesinski; *Administration:* Rita Brock, Karen Ladewig, Dolores Wangert, Janet Forbes, Chris Maynard; *Distribution Center:* James Haraughty.

Country Beautiful Corporation is a wholly owned subsidiary of Flick-Reedy Corporation: President: Frank Flick; Secretary-Treasurer: R. L. Robertson; Assistant Secretary-Treasurer: August Caamano.

ACKNOWLEDGEMENTS

The editors are grateful to the following publishers for permission to use the following material in this volume:

Excerpts from *Diving to Adventure* by Hans Hass translated by Barrows Mussey. Copyright 1951 by Doubleday & Company, Inc. and from *The Shark* copyright © 1970 by Jacques-Yves Cousteau. Reprinted by permission of Doubleday & Company, Inc.

Excerpt from "The Fish" from *The Complete Poems* by Elizabeth Bishop, © 1955 by Farrar, Straus & Giroux, Inc.

Excerpts from *Denizens of the Deep* by Philip Wylie reprinted by permission of Harold Ober Associates, Incorporated. Copyright © 1953 by Philip Wylie.

Excerpts from *The Living Sea* and *The Silent World* by Jacques-Yves Cousteau, reprinted by permission of Harper & Row, Publishers, Inc.

Excerpt from *The Living World of the Sea* by William J. Cromie, © 1966 by William J. Cromie. Published by Prentice-Hall, Inc., Englewood Cliffs, New Jersey.

Excerpts from *Kon-Tiki* by Thor Heyerdahl. Copyright 1950 by Thor Heyerdahl. Published in the United States by Rand McNally & Co.

Library of Congress Cataloging in Publication Data

John, Joseph, 1925-
    Lord of the sea.

    1. Sharks. I. Country beautiful. II. Title.
QL638.9.J68   597'.31   76-11780
ISBN 0-87294-085-3

CONTENTS

I Prologue: Man vs. Shark,
  Who Is the More Dangerous Predator? 7

II The Lord of the Sea 15

III The Gentle Giants 29

IV The Man-Eaters 45

V The Anatomy of the Consummate Killer 63

VI The Omnivore 73

VII Sharks and Men 83

VIII Epilogue 92

Appendix 94

"And what is the sea?" asked Will.

"The sea!" cried the miller. "Lord help us all, it is the greatest thing God made! ... There are great fish in it five times bigger than a bull, and one old serpent as long as our river and as old as all the world, with whiskers like a man, and a crown of silver on her head.

Robert Louis Stevenson
The Merry Men

Man vs. Shark
Who Is the More Dangerous Predator?

Today when man is poised for his exciting adventure into outer space, he is also on the threshold of a new era of exploration and conquest of the unknown and uncharted regions of the world's oceans. Even as we have our astronauts and cosmonauts, so we have oceanauts venturing into ocean depths considered inaccessible to man only a few years ago. And we have begun to think in terms of marine cities and farms of the future, of marine settlements that will ease the pressure on the earth's overpopulated land surface, of marine foods that will assuage the hunger of the world's "exploding" human population. In his effort to translate these visions into reality, man is bound to encounter, as never before, the "monsters of the deep" that have always struck terror in the human heart.

The "great fish" that the miller in the epigraph (left) describes with such homely inventiveness certainly include the shark. Indeed, the shark has been the most dreaded of all the sea creatures known to man. Man's fear of sharks has been expressed in different forms from the earliest times. In the bushland near Sydney, Australia, there is an aboriginal rock-carving depicting a hefty shark attacking a woman. In ancient Tahiti and Polynesia, the fear of the shark was sublimated into shark cults that wishfully transformed the predatory shark into a benign deity protecting its devotees from storms and other dangers at sea. One learned authority contends that the Biblical "fish" that swallowed Jonah must have been a squalus (shark) which alone, biologically speaking, could have accommodated the dissenting prophet within its leisurely belly for so long before belching him forth, all hale and hearty, at God's behest!

Fear of the shark is also reflected in man's naming of the different species of shark. Names such as "tiger shark" are patently suggestive, and in the French language the word for shark is *requin*, derived from Requiem, the Mass of the Dead. In almost every language, the shark has become a byword and a metaphor for predatoriness. And for a good many people acquainted with sharks either through books or movies or from personal experience as swimmers or divers, the shark is a visible symbol of man's nameless fear of the primordial unknown both within and beyond nature.

In his future attempts to colonize the seas, man is bound to find in the shark his most formidable adversary. He will not, to be sure, meet with fabulous serpents adorned with silver diadems, but he is sure to encounter gigantic sharks "five times bigger than a bull," and capable of reducing him to nothingness in a way a hundred bulls never could. Going out to sea with his inherited incubus of fear of, and hatred for, sharks, man may be tempted to seek shortcuts to security by using his superior intelligence and the drastic weapons it gives him to exterminate his foe from his natural habitat. Such a step will lead to disastrous consequences by upsetting the ocean's ecosystem. This is not to suggest that we allow ourselves to be possessed by romantic fascination or cultic veneration for the shark, but the situation does call for a change of attitude, a realistic appraisal of man's relation to the shark, which is likely to prove the most challenging obstacle to man's return to the sea. Such an appraisal will point not so much toward destruction as toward coexistence as an answer to the problem — a coexistence made possible by man himself

The sand shark, also known as the sand tiger shark, is commonly seen along the northeastern coast of the U.S. during summer months and can be encountered off Florida's eastern coast year-round. (Marineland of Florida)

The great blue shark is one of the most common and beautiful of the oceanic sharks. Its brilliant blue coloring on the upper portion of its body, however, fades rapidly with death. (U.S. Navy)

by virtue of his superior intelligence informed by a higher ethic that will no longer subscribe to regarding the shark as a convenient scape-goat for his own unsurpassed predatoriness.

While the tiger, the lion, the leopard, the crocodile, and the alligator have won due recognition as necessary beings in the order of creation, the shark still remains unexonerated as an implacable miscreant, a ruthless marauder whose species must be ruthlessly dealt with. The shark has yet to pass from the discreditable status of being *persona non grata* to *homo sapiens* to a new ecological recognition as a significant link in the chain of life on this planet. The new ecological ethic that seeks to leave behind man's outdated and indiscriminate violence and arrogant aggressiveness toward his non-human fellow creatures would demand that man, as the steward of God's creation or, at any rate, as the most intelligent avatar of the Life Force in its evolutionary ascent, must view the shark, a magnificent incarnation of the same Force, with the deference due to a creature whose evolutionary tenure on earth exceeds man's by several million years. Three hundred million years of intelligent survival on this planet is no mean record, when we think of the inexorable struggle for survival that has been the law of life in nature "red in tooth and claw," and when we recall the dinosaur, the mammoth, the dodo and other species that failed to prove themselves equal to the challenging task of survival. To have survived evolutionary eons as the shark has done demands intelligence of a kind that *homo sapiens* has not yet had time enough to show — his survival record being no more than roughly a million years. At a time like this, when the continuance of the human species is threatened more by man himself than by any other creature, it behooves us to try to understand the more ex-perienced of the earth's denizens such as the shark.

Part of this new understanding will consist in a frank recognition of the fact that man's "holier than thou" attitude in calling the shark a predator is sheer cant, if not hypocrisy. When it comes to predatoriness, man surely takes the palm, and the shark, though a runner-up, is not quite a close second. The shark kills only for food; man kills for pleasure also. He is probably the only creature that kills for pleasure, or sport, as he calls it, to glamorize his killer instinct. Though man is no longer cannibalistic, while the shark still is, man's worst enemy is man, even as the shark's worst enemy is his own kind. The shark has shown, through millions of years of survival as a species, that it has learned the secret of moderating intraspecific aggression so as to ensure the continuance of the species. It remains an open question whether man, with his infinitely more drastic means of intraspecific aggression and annihilation, will show the same instinctual wisdom in the years to come.

This wisdom must be rooted, not in knowledge, which man does not lack, but in sympathy and understanding, of which he needs to have more than he now has. This understanding will extend his compassionate concern to all his fellow creatures on earth including sharks, which are among the finest of nature's handiworks.

In recent years, there have been a number of investigators of shark life who have brought the light of this new ecological enlightenment to bear on their studies. D. K. Webster, a keen student of the shark and its ways, found it "one of nature's most fascinating, widely maligned, and least understood creatures." Philip Wylie, an experienced angler and observer of sharks, called it "that most misunderstood fish." He says that he has "swum cheek by jowl with various sharks of various weights and, to date, has suffered greater injury from mosquitoes." He adds that "it may be our shark-approach has been wrong for millenniums. Sharks are mechanized sets of teeth, sure. They can bite, beyond doubt. But . . . the word *shark* doesn't paralyze me and the sight of a periscopelike dorsal fin, gliding around where I am swimming, doesn't fill me with the sensation my last hour has come. Also, I don't kill all sharks on sight for no reason, as many deep-sea anglers do. . . . I've gradually found sharks a lot more interesting than horrifying."

Jacques Cousteau, with his years of underwater mingling with sharks of all kinds and sizes, says that they "rank among the most perfect, the most beautiful creatures ever developed in nature. We expect to meet them around coral reefs or in the open ocean, even if it is with a twist of fear. Their absence means disappointment for the divers, while their appearance is disquieting. When their formidable silhouette glides along the populated coral cliffs, fish do not panic; they quietly clear the lord's path, and keep an eye on him. So do we."

This is beyond me, this fish.
His God stands outside my God.

D. H. Lawrence, "Fish"

Master, I marvel how the fishes live in the sea.

Shakespeare, *Pericles*

The Lord of the Sea

Man, according to Jean-Paul Sartre, is a being "condemned to be free." An analogous definition of the shark would be: "a creature condemned to be in perpetual motion." Endlessly on the move from birth to death, forever at war with the law of gravity that would pull it down to the bottom the moment it stopped swimming, the shark is a creature whose very existence is motion, whose life is energy in action—energy indefatigable and all but inexhaustible.

Why does the shark have to keep moving, or sink? Because it does not have the air bladder (swim bladder) which functions in other fishes as a hydrostatic device, buoying them up against the force of gravity when not in motion and enabling them to move up and down as the bladder expands and contracts. Not having this device, the shark uses its own energy to keep itself from sinking as well as to ascend and descend. Its powerful tail and fins enable it to move forward and steer through the water at great speed.

In fact, sharks are among the swiftest swimmers in the sea. Even the supposedly sluggish species such as the Greenland shark can catch apparently more agile swimmers such as seals and salmon, and the whitetip shark, allegedly a slow swimmer, manages to feed on the reputedly much faster tuna. Some of the great speedsters among sharks attain remarkable speeds, as does the mako which, it has been estimated, can reach a speed of twenty-two knots.

Sharks differ from other fishes in more important ways, biologically speaking. First, unlike the majority of fishes which have bony skeletons, the shark's skeletal system consists entirely of cartilage. This supposedly represents arrested evolution: Bonyfishes are generally considered to represent an evolutionary stage ahead of the cartilaginous ones. However, considering that the shark's abode is water, it is hard to see how the more buoyant cartilage can be regarded as evolutionarily less advanced than the bone. It is quite probable that the shark's relatively lighter cartilaginous skeleton compensates, partially at least, for its having no air bladder.

Another remarkable thing about sharks is that, unlike most other fishes, they copulate and reproduce by internal fertilization. (Interestingly, this fact was noted more than two thousand years ago by Aristotle.) The sexual organ of the male shark consists of two long "claspers" which are introduced into openings in the cloaca of the female shark. The sperm cells are ejected into the oviduct of the female through the groove in each clasper. The females of most species give birth to living young: Only a minority of sharks lay eggs.

According to the manner in which offspring are produced, sharks are classified as oviparous, ovoviviparous, and viviparous. Oviparous sharks lay eggs, such as the whale shark, the cat shark, and the horn or bullhead shark. The young of ovoviviparous ones are developed and hatched from eggs inside the uterus of the mother before they are born alive. Among the ovoviviparous sharks are the frill shark, the goblin shark, the saw shark, and the mako shark. Female viviparous sharks give birth to young, not hatched from eggs within the uterus, but developed as in the mammalian female. The tiger shark, the great blue shark, the lemon shark, the basking shark, and the spiny dogfishes are among those that belong to this category.

Scientists believe that all sharks must have once belonged to an egg-laying group. Later, some of them became ovoviviparous by

Only a minority of sharks lay eggs. The shape of egg cases varies from rectangular to conical, but most have tendrils in their corners that serve as anchors. Laid in pairs, the eggs hatch in six to ten months. (Rondi Church)

retaining the eggs within the body. Others developed a placenta-like structure inside which the embryo was nourished. Thus the sharks evolved farther than other fishes in their reproductive modes, while they have retained their "primitive" cartilaginous skeletal system for billions of years. They are, therefore, a "living contradiction," an object of great interest to biologists.

Quite an obvious difference between sharks and most other fishes is that the shark's skin is covered, not with scales, but with what are called denticles which, as the name indicates, are modified, though minuscule, forms of its own teeth. Reinforced with such formidable material, the shark's skin is incredibly tough and abrasive, as divers and others who have come into contact with it, have testified.

Passing from denticles to dentures, the shark has been credited with having "pioneered" an evolutionary breakthrough by being the first animal to develop teeth. Since then, it has not let any other creature excel or even equal it in the lethal power and abundance of its dental weaponry.

As one of the hoariest evolutionary "oldtimers" on the planet, the shark is a tough creature uniquely adapted to survive the vicissitudes of the ages. Sharks have, as Wylie says, "adapted themselves to all sorts of conditions — varying water temperature, countless sorts of food, and, as few people know, even to *fresh* water. There is a body of fresh water [in Central America] known as Lake Nicaragua which contains not only sharks but skates and rays. The lake was once probably a part of the sea; volcanic action closed it off; tributaries gradually diluted its salt content until today it is entirely fresh. But the dilution was slow and the shark population had time to adjust. It did. So it's hard to kill a shark even by geological means!"

In terms of sheer physical toughness, perhaps no other creature can rival the shark. "Why doesn't anything seem to hurt you, Mr. Jaws?" is no idle question, as witness the following account by Jacques Cousteau:

> We saw a fifteen-foot nurse shark. I summoned Didi and conveyed to him in sign language that he would be permitted to relax our neutrality toward sharks and take a crack at this one with his super-harpoon gun. It had a six-foot spear with an explosive head and three hundred pounds of traction in its elastic bands. Dumas fired straight down at a distance of twelve feet. The four-pound harpoon struck the shark's head and, two seconds later, the harpoon tip exploded. We were severely shaken. There was some pain involved.
>
> The shark continued to swim away, imperturbably, with the spear sticking from its head like a flagstaff. After a few strokes the harpoon shaft fell to the bottom and the shark moved on. We swam after it as fast as we could to see what would happen. The shark showed every sign of normal movement, accelerated gradually and vanished. The only conclusion we could draw was that the harpoon went clear through the head and exploded externally, because no internal organ could survive a blast that nearly incapacitated us two harpoon lengths away. Even so, taking such a burst a few inches from the head demonstrated the extraordinary vitality of sharks.

Another story related by Philip Wylie provides an equally impressive instance of the shark's stupendous endurance against the utmost physical punishment:

How hard it is to kill one by hand and in person is testified by Captain Art Wills of the *Sea Queen* — a charterboat berthed at Miami Beach. On a Bimini fishing expedition, the *Sea Queen* "raised" a mako shark. The big fish gave the angler the fight of his life but, after something over two hours, was brought to gaff.

"We got a tail rope on the mako," Captain Wills once told me, "and heaved him aboard. He was a big one, well over four hundred. Still full of fight. I clubbed him with a heavy billy—often and hard enough to kill a dozen blue marlin. He still had a wiggle left. So I broke out an ice pick and stabbed him, by actual count, twenty-three times, in what I thought was the brain at every clip—and what I was sure would be the brain, in twenty-three tries. Then I lashed him with new rope across the stern. His head hung overboard on one side of the boat, his tail on the other. We started in. And all of a sudden I saw that mako begin to tense himself against the rope."

Captain Wills is a sanguine man, as a rule. I've seen him merely chuckle when two hundrend and fifty pounds of blue marlin (on my line) charged into the stern of the *Sea Queen* and drove his bill deep into the mahogany. At this moment, however, Art Wills admits he was excited:

"One of the rope strands snapped! I couldn't believe it! Luckily the mako had swallowed the bait and we'd left the hook, leader and line where it was. Nobody in his right mind would reach into even a presumably dead mako's mouth to get back a hook! I yelled at the passenger who'd caught the mako to grab his rod and get back in the fighting chair—just in case. Good thing. The 'in case' was fact, seconds later. That beat-up, stabbed, 'dead' mako gave one enormous heave, snapped all the line around it and went overboard." Captain Wills paused here and shook his head as if he hardly believed it himself. "We had to fish the fish all over again. It took another *hour* before the angler could bring him to gaff a second time. When he did, we made doggone sure we wouldn't lose him overboard again. We lashed him

under the canopy and we not only disconnected his brain from the rest
of him with a knife, but we sat on him all the way in!"

That's a pretty high score in viability — the sheer power to stay
alive.

Sharks have been known to stay alive for a considerable length
of time even after the head has been cut off. W. S. Berridge cites the
story of a great blue shark that, when thrown back into the sea after
being "beheaded," swam around for quite some time. If this story
sounds apocryphal, there is the incontrovertible evidence provided
by Jacques Cousteau's account of a similar event:

On deck our men had watched them [the sharks] devouring the
whale and were overcome with the hatred of sharks that lies so close
under the skin of a sailor. When we finished filming, the crew ran
around grabbing anything with which they could punish a shark—
crowbars, fire axes, gaffs, and tuna hooks—and they got down onto
the diving platform to thrust, knock, slash, and hook sharks. They
hauled flipping sharks onto the deck in a production line and finished
them off. Delmas yelled, "Death to the blue!" and hauled the big blue
shark on board. Dumas sat on a dead one, already eviscerated, and cut
its head off to collect the jaw. When he tossed the body over the side,
the headless shark swam away.

The hatred of sharks that Cousteau mentions has much to do
with what Edward R. Ricciuti calls the "spectral shark" which lurks
far back in man's consciousness as the symbol of all the primordial

fears that civilized man believes he has long since left behind. Movies like *Jaws* and *The Exorcist* probably owe their immense popularity to the fact that they provided a vicarious means of "exorcising" these nameless fears.

Nowhere among nature's larger creatures is the contrast between the abysmally primitive and the self-consciously sophisticated so pronounced as in the polarity between shark and man. The shark is the ultimate antithesis to man: Having taken, as it were, a multibillion-year holiday from the evolutionary process, it is a primeval, piscine behemoth, an anachronistic minion of the Mesozoic age guarding its marine dominion against man, the proud architect of the space era, with his eyes trained on the galaxies, his mind set on unraveling the ocean's mysteries. The shark has retained its gigantic size and strength without acquiring the physio-psychic complexification which, in its most sophisticated form, has placed man at the apex of the evolutionary pyramid. But what the shark has lost in selective complexification it has gained in effective simplification as the perfect predator: It is instinct incarnate—its entire being intensely alive to the ocean's circumambient contingencies, all its energies merging into a relentless rectilinear thrust toward self-preservation and survival. The shark revels in the glory of being itself. Like William Blake's tiger ("Tiger! Tiger! burning bright"), it is beyond good and evil, and it makes its way through the water as though it were a law and a power sufficient unto itself.

The shark's lordly passage through the water is "cleared" by a "liveried" retinue of zebra-striped pilot fish that swim just ahead of his great snout, but not close enough to be snapped up by him. These pilot fish are lowly hangers-on thriving on bits and scraps from their master's hefty meals; they are not, as they were once thought to be,

With perhaps half a dozen exceptions, all sharks are carnivorous,
normally feeding on other fishes and invertebrates. A popular misconception
is that a shark must roll over on its back to seize its prey.
(Marineland of Florida)

guides leading their supposedly purblind lord to his prey. The proverbial "loyalty" of these humble vassals to the lordly shark has been noted by every seaman or diver who has witnessed the phenomenon. Going wherever the shark goes, these pilot fish behave as if in fealty bound to their lord and master. If the shark takes a leap into the air, they will wait and promptly take up their accustomed position as soon as he descends into the water. Imagine their bewilderment when, on occasion, the "lord" fails to come down after going up. This occurs when a shark is hooked up aboard at the end of a line. What happens when the humble entourage of a shark is thus "orphaned" has been described by Thor Heyerdahl:

> Then the pilot fish scurried about in a distracted manner, searching wildly, but always came back and wriggled along astern of the raft, where the shark had vanished skyward. But as time passed and the shark did not come down again, they had to look round for a new lord and master. And none was nearer to hand than the *Kon-Tiki* herself.
>
> If we let ourselves down over the side of the raft, with our heads down in the brilliantly clear water, we saw the raft as the belly of a sea monster, with the steering oar as its tail and the centerboards hanging down like blunt fins. In between them all the adopted pilot fish swam, side by side, and took no notice of the bubbling human head except that one or two of them darted swiftly aside and peered right up its nose, only to wriggle back again unperturbed and take their places in the ranks of eager swimmers.

Another lowly ocean dweller to whom the shark plays host, however unwittingly, is the remora, or shark sucker, which attaches itself tightly to the shark's body by means of a sucking disc at the top

*Remoras, fish that can reach four feet in length, have a disk
on top of their heads that provides strong suction. Attaching themselves to sharks,
they consume tiny parasites on their host's skin. (Marineland of Florida)*

of its head. So tight is its hold on the shark's skin that it is virtually impossible to pull it off by the tail. In the absence of a shark to suck itself on to, the remora will find a temporary substitute in another fish. Fishermen in tropical seas sometimes use remoras to catch bigger fish. Tied to the end of a line and thrown into the sea, the remora quickly attaches itself to the first fish that comes along and, when it does so, is hauled aboard with its newfound "host." Philippe Cousteau reports how remoras collected from sharks' bodies were profitably used by tribal islanders of the Mozambique Channel. The remoras used by these fishermen, says Cousteau, "often attached themselves to others of the large fish or to the turtles in which these waters abound, and the hosts they had selected were then hauled in and sold." The same method was tried by members of the *Kon-Tiki* expedition, but with no luck. "Every single time we let a remora go with a line tied to its tail," says Thor Heyerdahl, "it simply shot off and sucked itself fast to one of the logs of the raft, in the belief that it had found an extrafine big shark. And there it hung, however hard we tugged on the line. We gradually acquired a number of these small remoras which hung on and dangled obstinately among the shells on the side of the raft, traveling with us right across the Pacific."

The big shark goes about with a full complement of pilot fish and remoras and other parasites in its entourage so that the whole set-up looks, as Thor Heyerdahl observed, like a "curious zoological collection crowded round something that resembled a floating deep-water reef." For the layman who is neither a scuba diver nor a maritime adventurer the next best thing to actually witnessing this interesting phenomenon at sea is to see it on the screen in movies such as *Blue Water, White Death.*

The shark is an important "personage" in the hierarchy of life in the piscine kingdom. Life in the ocean would be as much the poorer without sharks as life on land would be without lions, tigers or elephants. The shark's role in the ecology of the ocean is of extreme importance. Because they are predominantly piscivorous, sharks play an essential part in trimming down the "population" of several species of fish in the ocean so as to keep their numbers within the limits of the ocean's capacity to support and sustain them. In addition, the members of the large schools of fish that the shark usually preys on are the weaker ones unfit for survival, and their elimination serves a useful purpose in strengthening the species to which they belong. As the dominant predators in an environment where mutual predation is the law of life, sharks must have, over the years, played a decisive role in determining the adaptive changes in the biological and behavioral evolution of myriads of other species of fish.

Any substantial reduction in the number of sharks in the wake of man's colonization of the seas will upset the balance of life in the world of fishes. This will lead to a major ecological disaster that will ultimately recoil upon human life. It is important, therefore, that man's approach to the shark be informed by the new ecological ethic that points to the need for coexistence with sharks rather than their partial or wholesale extermination and calls upon man to refrain from seeking to reduce the life of the shark to a few conveniently isolated "reservations" in the vastness of the marine world.

'Twas my heart-cherished wish for to slay many fish
Each day did my malice grow worse,
For my heart didn't soften with doing it so often,
But rather, I should say, the reverse.

Lewis Carroll, "The Two Brothers"

Fishing, if I, a fisher, may protest
Of pleasures is the sweet'st, of sports the best,
Of exercises the most excellent,
Of Recreations the most innocent,
But now the sport is marred, and wot ye why?
Fishes decrease, and fishers multiply.

Reverend Thomas Bastard
Chrestoleros, 1598

The Gentle Giants

Coexistence between man and shark will pose no serious problems in regard to the great majority of sharks. Not every shark is dangerous to man. Of the more than two hundred and fifty known species of shark, only about twenty may be considered dangerous, and of these twenty, no more than five or six can be considered man-eaters with any degree of certainty. The largest of the sharks, the whale shark, which is also the largest fish (the still larger whale being a mammal), is a gentle leviathan that poses no threat to man. Second only to the whale shark in size, the basking shark is another peaceful giant whom man has no reason to fear. In fact, because of their peaceful nature, these two giants often become victims of man's cupidity, greed, and perversity.

The two largest species of shark are gentle and docile creatures. Only about eight percent of the many species of shark are of any real threat to man, a fact that often goes unnoticed amidst the furore caused by the sensational activities of a few predatory culprits whose occasional forays into beaches and other inshore waters hit the headlines of national newspapers. Thus the popular misconception that all sharks are ferocious man-eaters scouring the waters for human quarry is kept alive.

WHALE SHARK

The whale shark is a fascinating creature. Its gentleness, for all its incredible size, has always intrigued man and perhaps always will. Found mostly in equatorial and tropical seas, it may grow up to a maximum size of seventy-five feet. Strangely enough, this giant feeds solely on plankton and small fish. To eat these, all it has to do is to propel itself through the water with its mouth wide open, imbibing large quantities of water along with the plankton and fish that abound in it. The water goes out through the gills, while the plankton and fish pass into its huge belly. Sometimes this giant performs an underwater acrobatic stunt by standing upright in order to gulp shoals of fish moving past its gaping mouth.

Resting on the surface for long stretches of time, whale sharks are occasionally hit by ocean liners on the high seas. But generally these great fish prefer the ocean depths where plankton, of which they are so fond, abounds. It is believed that they come to the surface when the plankton is carried upward by the current. Because of their preference for the ocean depths, sightings of whale sharks by seamen are relatively rare — so rare that their appearance, when it does occur, causes quite a commotion aboard.

The following account, by Thor Heyerdahl, of an encounter with a whale shark on the famed *Kon-Tiki* expedition gives some idea of the excitement caused by the appearance of this great fish:

. . . It was May 24, and we were lying drifting on a leisurely swell in exactly 95° west by 7° south. It was about noon, and we had thrown overboard the guts of the two big dolphins we had caught earlier in the morning. I was having a refreshing plunge overboard at the bow, lying in the water but keeping a good lookout and hanging on to a rope end, when I caught sight of a thick brown fish, six feet long, which came swimming inquisitively toward me through the crystal-clear sea water. I hopped quickly up on to the edge of the raft and sat in the hot sun looking at the fish as it passed quietly,when I heard a wild war whoop from Knut, who was sitting aft behind the bamboo cabin. He bellowed, "Shark!" till his voice cracked in a falsetto, and, as we had sharks swimming alongside the raft almost daily without creating such excitement, we all realized that this must be something extra-special and flocked astern to Knut's assistance.

Knut had been squatting there, washing his pants in the swell, and when he looked up for a moment he was staring straight into the biggest and ugliest face any of us had ever seen in the whole of our lives. It was the head of a veritable sea monster, so huge and hideous that, if the Old Man of the Sea himself had come up, he could not have made such an impression on us. The head was broad and flat like a frog's, with two small eyes right at the sides, and a toadlike jaw which was four or five feet wide and had long fringes drooping from the cor-ners of the mouth. Behind the head was an enormous body ending in a long thin tail with a pointed tail fin which stood straight up and show-ed that this sea monster was not any kind of whale. The body looked brownish under the water, but both head and body were thickly covered with small white spots.

The monster came quietly, lazily swimming after us from astern. It grinned like a bulldog and lashed gently with its tail. The large round dorsal fin projected clear of the water and sometimes the tail fin as well, and, when the creature was in the trough of the swell, the water flowed about the broad back as though washing round a submerged reef....

A twenty-five pound dolphin, attached to six of our largest fish-hooks, was hanging behind the raft as bait for sharks, and a swarm of the pilot fish shot straight off, nosed the dolphin without touching it, and then hurried back to their lord and master, the sea king. Like a mechanical monster it set its machinery going and came gliding at leisure toward the dolphin which lay, a beggarly trifle, before its jaws.

We tried to pull the dolphin in, and the sea monster followed slowly, right up to the side of the raft. It did not open its mouth but just let the dolphin bump against it, as if to throw open the whole door for such an insignificant scrap was not worth while. When the giant came close up to the raft, it rubbed its back against the heavy steering oar, which was just lifted up out of the water, and now we had ample opportunity of studying the monster at the closest quarters — at such close quarters that I thought we had all gone mad, for we roared stupidly with laughter and shouted overexcitedly at the completely fantastic sight we saw. Walt Disney himself, with all his powers of imagination, could not have created a more hair-raising sea monster than that which thus suddenly lay with its terrific jaws along the raft's side.

The monster was a whale shark, the largest shark and the largest fish known in the world today. It is exceedingly rare, but scattered specimens are observed here and there in the tropical oceans. The whale shark has an average length of fifty feet, and according to zoologists it weighs fifteen tons. It is said that large specimens can attain a length of sixty feet; one harpooned baby had a liver weighing six hundred pounds and a collection of three thousand teeth in each of its broad jaws.

Our monster was so large that, when it began to swim in circles round us and under the raft, its head was visible on one side while the whole of its tail stuck out on the other. And so incredibly grotesque, inert, and stupid did it appear when seen fullface that we could not stop shouting with laughter, although we realized that it had strength enough in its tail to smash both balsa logs and ropes to pieces if it attacked us. Again and again it described narrower and narrower circles just under the raft, while all we could do was to wait and see what might happen. When it appeared on the other side, it glided amiably under the steering oar and lifted it up in the air, while the oar blade slid along the creature's back.

We stood round the raft with hand harpoons ready for action, but they seemed to us like toothpicks in relation to the mammoth beast we had to deal with. There was no indication that the whale shark ever thought of leaving us again; it circled round us and followed like a faithful dog, close up to the raft. None of us had ever experienced or thought we should experience anything like it; the whole adventure, with the sea monster swimming behind and under the raft, seemed to us so completely unnatural that we could not really take it seriously.

In reality the whale shark went on encircling us for barely an hour, but to us the visit seemed to last a whole day. At last it became too exciting for Erik, who was standing at a corner of the raft with an eight-foot hand harpoon, and, encouraged by ill-considered shouts, he raised the harpoon above his head. As the whale shark came gliding slowly toward him and its broad head moved right under the corner of the raft, Erik thrust the harpoon with all his giant strength down between his legs and deep into the whale shark's gristly head. It was a second or two before the giant understood properly what was happening. Then in a flash the placid half-wit was transformed into a mountain of steel muscles.

We heard a swishing noise as the harpoon line rushed over the edge of the raft and saw a cascade of water as the giant stood on its head and plunged down into the depths. The three men who were standing nearest were flung about the place, head over heels, and two of them were flayed and burned by the line as it rushed through the air. The thick line, strong enough to hold a boat, was caught up on the side of the raft but snapped at once like a piece of twine, and a few seconds later a broken-off harpoon shaft came up to the surface two hundred yards away. A shoal of frightened pilot fish shot off through the water in a desperate attempt to keep up with their old lord and master. We waited a long time for the monster to come racing back like an infuriated submarine, but we never saw anything more of him.

Heyerdahl's description brings out the awe and wonder he and his crew felt at the gigantic proportions of their visitor from the depths. However, the sensitive reader will have felt that the attack on the gentle fish was totally uncalled for. In the opinion of shark experts, when a whale shark draws near to a ship or any other craft, it does so simply out of curiosity, and with no aggressive intent. According to ichthyologist E. W. Gudger, the whale shark has "absolutely no offensive habits." The shark here described makes no aggressive gesture: It merely circles the *Kon-Tiki*, curiously observing it. But man's immemorial animus against brute creation, or rather, an atavistic response of the brute within man to the brute without, stirs in Erik's breast at the sight of the shark's awesome immensity, and, amidst the misguided applause of his fellows, he plunges an eight-foot harpoon into the majestic creature's head. Notwithstanding his size and strength and his tremendous capacity to do damage, the attacked shark simply removes itself from within reach of the aggressor. Its behavior confirms Gudger's observation that the whale shark is "entirely lacking" in defensive response when attacked. Because of its docility, the whale shark has been used by enterprising showmen who, advertising it as a killer, have hoodwinked spectators with the "daredevil" feat of riding on its back.

Stories of man's aggression on these harmless giants abound. To attack them on sight with guns or harpoons has been the rule rather than the exception with seamen, explorers and adventurers. Gudger himself has related several of such unprovoked attacks. In his book, *Animal Kingdom*, William Beebe describes a similar assault on another harmless member of the same species. In all these cases, what is remarkable is the picture evoked, not necessarily by authorial design, of man as the aggressor and the shark, giant though he is, as victim.

Fortunately, happier encounters between man and the whale shark are also on record—encounters in which both man and shark are led by peaceful, even friendly, curiosity about each other. One such encounter is described in *The Shark: Splendid Savage of the Sea* by Jacques Cousteau:

Sunday, May 7, 11:30 A.M. The *Calypso* was cruising at ten knots, between Mombasa and Djibouti. At this time of year, the Indian Ocean, where it borders the coast of Africa, is still calm. The famous southwest monsoon is already assembling its forces, but has not yet attacked. The surface of the water reflects disturbing tropical clouds, but there has been no indication of life to attract our attention since the day before. Not the smallest school of bonito, not a single flying fish, and no sign of the blowing of a whale. . . .

At eleven thirty-five, Pierre Li on the port watch noticed something in the water and called it to the attention of the bridge. A few moments later Captain Roger Maritano ordered the helm to port, and the *Calypso* was on her way to track down the object. At first, we could make out only two large fins, separated from each other by a distance of many feet, but there could be no doubt that this was a very large animal. Soon, it became evident that it was not a species of marine mammal. It appeared, in fact, to be an enormous shark, half asleep on the surface. A pilgrim shark or a whale shark? We knew very little of either. The pilgrim shark is an impressive specimen, sometimes attaining a length of thirty feet. He makes an appearance in the Mediterranean during the spring (generally in April), traveling in little groups and swimming lazily on the surface. Then he disappears, and no one knows exactly where or how he lives during the rest of the year. But the whale shark is by far the largest and heaviest living fish of our time — if one bears in mind that the whale itself is not a fish, but a mammal. The whale shark is a pure shark, and only his size justifies his descriptive name. This giant likes warm and very deep waters, and comes to the surface very, very seldom. An encounter with him is a rare event indeed. . . .

Excitement aboard the ship was intense. The *Zodiac* was put into the water within a few minutes, and the cameramen, Barsky and

Deloire, and the divers, Falco and Coll, leaped into it. They made a noiseless approach to the somnolent animal, and the divers slipped into the water. The shark's tail was very tall and very long, the dorsal fin massive and rounded — it was actually a whale shark! He seemed interested by the *Zodiac*, and began to swim very slowly around it. He was about thirty-five feet long. Deloire swam closer, trying to film him with an undersea camera provided with a wide-angle lens. The enormous animal presented his profile first, and then came straight toward the camera. His open jaw resembled the forward end of a jet engine on an airliner. When he was no more than five feet away from Deloire, he suddenly submerged, just enough to pass beneath the diver. Coll, for his part, had equipped himself with his famous banderilla, with which he had already marked so many other sharks. He dived with the monster, and dived again; each time he was out-distanced he would climb back on board the *Zodiac*. When the little boat caught up with the shark, Coll dived once more. When he emerged from the water for the last time, he described what had happened, in his usual laconic terms:

"The caudal fin is six and a half feet, from end to end. The dorsal is a little over four feet at its base and almost four feet in height. The eyes are round, slightly slanted, and very alert. He sees very well. Twice, he came back for another look at the *Zodiac*, and each time that we approached him from in front, he lowered his head a little and passed beneath us. We saw him dive several times: he begins by inclining gently toward the bottom and goes deeper, in the manner of a submarine, but when he does this he comes back to the surface a few minutes later and just a little farther away. But when he had had enough of playing with us, he just swung over to a vertical axis and disappeared, straight down, like a sounding whale. I held on to his tail several times, and he did not react at all — either to attack or to defend himself. His skin is rough and covered with round spots, hard to see. There were remoras clinging to his skin almost everywhere, especially behind the branchial clefts. There is a cavity there, where they go in and come out. There was only one pilot fish with him, a striped one. I

*The black-tip, receiving its name from the darker shade coloring the
tips of its fins, lives in schools in tropical and subtropical seas of the Pacific and
Atlantic oceans. (Marineland of Florida)*

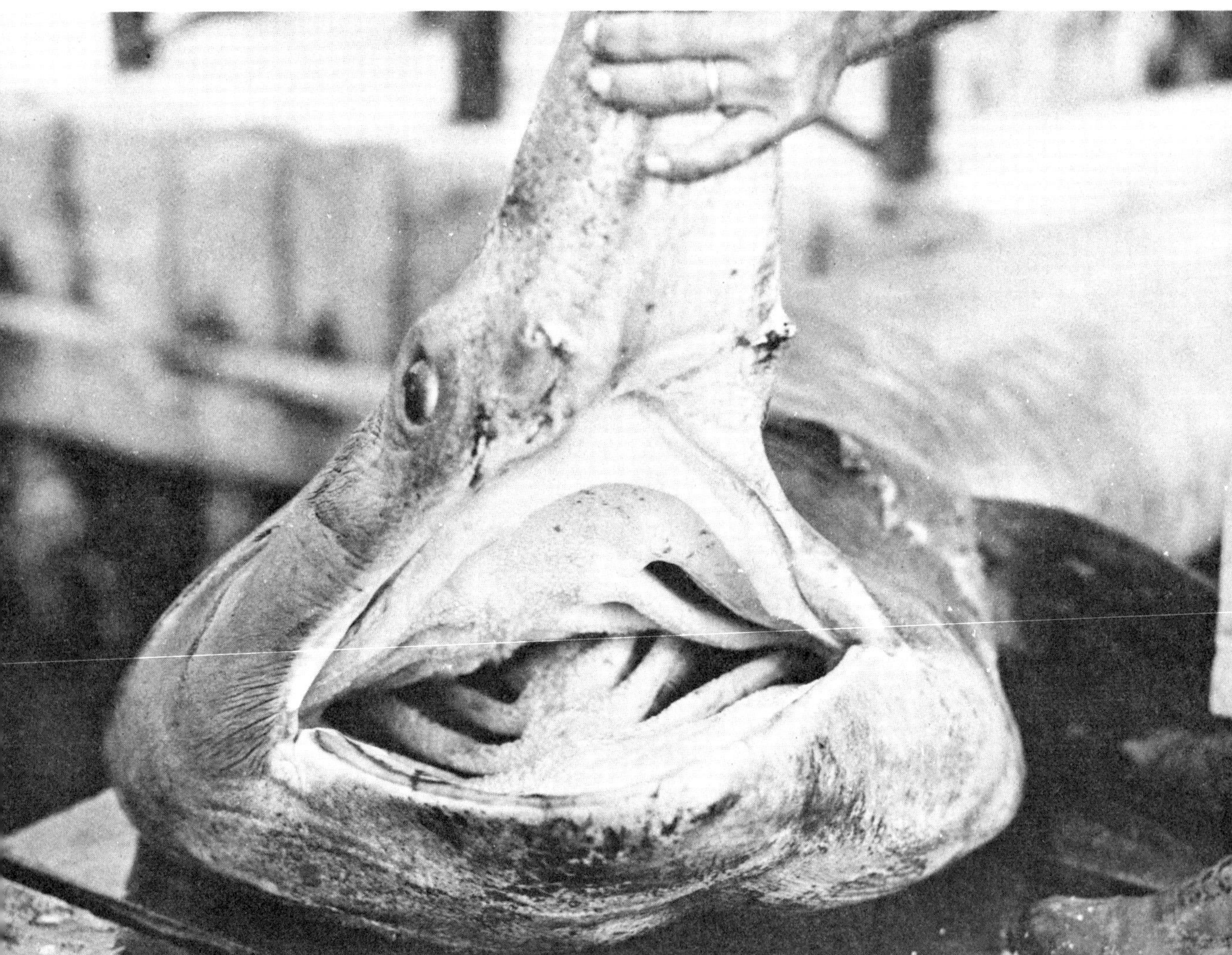

The basking shark is one of the gentler species. Though they range in size from 24 to 40 feet, their numerous tiny teeth and slow movement pose little threat to man. (Marineland of Florida)

had trouble planting a plaque near his dorsal fin; the skin is very hard to pierce and I twisted the point of the spear."

A few minutes later, a second specimen of the same species appeared, an even larger one than the first. This one measured forty to fifty feet. Number Two, as we christened him, did not stay with us as long as his predecessor, but Coll succeeded in marking him and then, clinging to his dorsal fin, was dragged down with him as he plunged into the depths. Coll stayed with him to a depth of almost a hundred and fifty feet.

"At no time," he told me later, "did he even attempt to escape or to get rid of me. His only reaction occurred when we came into his line of vision, and the reaction was curiosity. . . ."

The completely different responses of Heyerdahl and his men and of Cousteau and his crew to their marine visitor are indicative of the dissimilar orientations of the maritime adventurer and of the scientific explorer — the former insensitive to the life force that dwells alike in man and beast, the latter conscious of the fellowship of life that binds man to all living things.

BASKING SHARK

Only one other shark, the basking shark, rivals the whale shark in being absolutely docile and peaceful. Though not as gigantic as the whale shark, the basking shark is a giant all the same, with its immense size ranging between twenty-five and forty-five feet. Generally, it is a denizen of the temperate and subarctic regions of the Atlantic and Pacific oceans. Its food habits are similar to those of the whale shark: Plankton and crustaceans are its main diet. Because of its basking habit, it too, like the whale shark, sometimes gets hit by a ship. Why does it bask? The question has intrigued everyone who has observed this habitual "basker." Some have suggested that it is probably "sunbathing," but this cannot be a complete explanation, since it has been seen basking in cloudy or rainy weather as well. Indeed, no completely satisfactory explanation has been given by anyone. At any rate, for the basking shark itself, it is a costly habit, making it an easy victim of human predators and of possible collision with man-made craft. As D. K. Webster puts it, "Unaccustomed to fighting and having no natural foe (except, perhaps, the killer whale), it meets man as the first Indian met the whites, placidly; and like the Indian, it is rewarded with death."

THRESHER SHARK

Another big shark that is harmless to man is the thresher shark found in both warm and temperate seas. A minor giant of about twenty feet in size, and with an enormous tail nearly as long as its body, the thresher shark makes good use of its extra long tail by threshing the water with it while circling a school of fish which are thus rounded up to form a convenient bunch for it to feed on.

NURSE SHARK

The nurse shark is another species that man need not be afraid of. It feeds primarily on crustaceans. Like the whale and basking sharks, it is a docile creature. "You can actually swim up to a huge nurse shark and give it a kick," says Dr. Eugenie Clark, an experienced diving biologist, "and it will only swim away from you. This is the type you normally see in the movies when a 'courageous' man dives underwater, grabs hold of a shark, and stabs the poor

Catfishlike in appearance, the nurse shark has fleshy barbels in front of its nostrils. It is one of the few sharks whose skin is smooth to the touch. (Marineland of Florida)

harmless creature in the belly." For its amiable disposition, the Tahitians affectionately call it "Nohipiri."

There are many sharks that do not retaliate against human attacks, but there are several others that do. Even these latter, however, attack humans only when provoked. We have the testimony of Jacques Cousteau who says, "It is indisputable that many swimmers and many shipwrecked people have been bitten or killed. But to my knowledge there has been no documentation proving that deep divers have been wounded by unprovoked attacks — the divers themselves may have been guilty of what might be termed a lack of proper behavior." Philip Wylie, speaking of shark bites, says that "in every case, the man bitten had first shoved, socked, swatted, struck or tried to harpoon the shark! A little shark . . . , assaulted by a human being, can and sometimes does turn around and bite his assailant. A mouse does the same thing exactly." Divers who are not guilty of a "lack of proper behavior" seldom come to harm from sharks, as attested to by the experience of such a veteran diver as Jacques Cousteau who has survived more than three decades of deep-sea diving and oceanic expeditions "in the company of sharks: all kinds of sharks, sharks of every disposition, sharks reputed to be harmless, and sharks known to be deadly." There is much truth in Wylie's statement that "if sharks were as reckless and rampaging as they are imagined to be, deep sea diving would be out of the question." And it is probably true, as Jacques Cousteau points out, that diving even in the shark-infested waters of the tropics is "actually much less dangerous than riding a motorcycle."

The ocean is a wilderness reaching round the globe, wilder than a Bengal jungle, and fuller of monsters, washing the very wharves of our cities and the gardens of our seaside residences. Serpents, bears, hyenas, tigers, rapidly vanish as civilization advances, but the most populous and civilized city cannot scare a shark far from its wharves.

Henry David Thoreau, *Cape Cod*

At that very moment they looked, and lo, the dog-catcher was approaching.

The three dogs sprang up and scampered down the street; and as they ran the third dog said, "For God's sake, run for your lives. Civilization is after us."

Kahlil Gibran, "Peace and War"

The Man-Eaters

Cousteau's assurances about the relative safety of diving in shark-infested waters should not be construed as suggesting that man can merrily mingle with sharks unconcerned about any danger from them. Such complacency could be fatal, for there are known man-eaters among sharks. Do sharks have a special craving for human flesh? Normally, of course, they are satisfied with their customary diet, but if a human victim comes in handy, they are not averse to adding the rare item to their menu. Calling the shark a man-eater signifies that, given the opportunity, it will, with alacrity, dine on human flesh.

Strangely enough, such opportunities have often been given to the shark by man himself. Superstitious primitives in bygone times have offered human sacrifices to sharks considered to be benevolent deities. Scheming and cruel-hearted villains have often disposed of their enemies by throwing them to hungry sharks. The kings of ancient Hawaii and Polynesia are known to have used human flesh as the proper bait for the "sacred" shark — a royal custom that well served the Machiavellian politics of those island despots by giving a religious touch to their tactical decision to "honor" a troublesome subject by choosing him as human bait. Unscrupulous slave smugglers have often, on being approached by British vessels policing the seas, thrown their hapless slaves overboard to ship-trailing sharks in order to escape prosecution. A ruthless slave trader once halted an alarming wave of suicide among his slaves by simply lowering the body of the latest suicide by rope into the shark-filled sea and,

after a few seconds, pulling up the defleshed skeleton in full view of
the remaining slaves who were thus dissuaded from killing
themselves, as the others had done, in the fond hope of being
restored by death to their people back in Africa. The hundreds of
shipwrecked seamen and downed airmen who were eaten by sharks
during the two world wars have added substantially to man's con-
tribution to the shark's occasional human diet. However, no shark
ever gets the chance to subsist entirely on human flesh.

GREAT WHITE SHARK

The shark with the most gruesome reputation as a man-eater is,
beyond doubt, the great white shark. Next only to the whale shark
and the basking shark in size, it is a man-eater that grows up to about
thirty-five feet in size. In 1918, David Stead recorded the appearance
in Australian waters of a great white shark of enormous dimensions
that struck terror in the hearts of fishermen. So huge was the fish
that those who saw it, in their confusion, variously imagined its size
to be between one hundred and fifteen feet and three hundred!
Sinister in appearance and capable of unprovoked attacks, the
great white shark has been the terror of sailors from the time man
first took to the sea. Unwary seamen aboard becalmed ships have
been dragged down to the depths by the "white death" (as this shark
is often called) reaching out unexpectedly from the dark water.
There are recorded instances of white sharks, without any provocation, charging into boats and skiffs like a torpedo or like a bull infuriated by a red rag.
Although it is a pelagic fish, living in the open sea, the white
shark occasionally raids inshore waters or combs the beaches for

The great white shark also goes by the chilling name of White Death.
Its large, serrated teeth and tendency to attack without provocation lends credibility
to its reputation as a ferocious aggressor. (Marineland of Florida)

prey, leaving behind a trail of human blood and tragedy. White sharks have, now and then, been found in the shallowest of waters. A man was once chased by a white shark in knee-deep water.

According to Victor Coppleson, a shark may develop a taste for human flesh after tasting it once. It might have been such a shark that caused the great New Jersey shark scare in July 1916. The villain of this story, which is perhaps the most sensational event in shark annals, was a great white shark which claimed headlines in national newspapers by a series of fatal attacks on humans along the New Jersey coast in just ten days.

The ferocity of the great white shark is almost legendary. The entire jaw of a white shark was once found embedded in the timber of a sailing clipper: The shark had bitten so hard into it that it could not withdraw its teeth! The great white shark has been known to smash boats and other vessels by virtue of its immense size and strength. In 1953, a white shark measuring about twelve feet attacked a fourteen-foot dory off Cape Breton Island, Nova Scotia. The dory was damaged and one of its two occupants was drowned.

The white shark is also known for the fury with which it retaliates when harassed or provoked. Theo W. Brown, well-known shark expert and author of *Sharks: The Silent Savages*, mentions the case of a white shark that smashed the diving platform of his boat to the accompaniment of a great deal of "sharky" rigmarole in the form of angry sounds emanating from the creature's marauding mouth.

For all its savagery and reckless aggressiveness, the white shark sometimes behaves as though it believed, as did Falstaff, that discretion is the better part of valor. Jacques Cousteau reports that he and

As many as five rows of teeth lie flat beneath the folds of the gum in a shark. When one of the upright, outer teeth is lost or damaged, a reserve tooth moves up to replace it. (Marineland of Florida)

The tiger shark receives its common name from dark, irregular bars or "stripes" located on its sides and fins which are easily identifiable in the younger specimens. (U.S. Navy)

his fellow-diver, Dumas, once got the fright of their lives when they saw a great white shark not far from where they were in deep ocean. Even as the two divers drew closer to each other in fear of the shark, the dreaded monster, noticing the presence of the humans, vamoosed instantly, leaving behind the stench of ordure from its suddenly emptied bowels! Diving biologist Donald R. Nelson has another story that shows how the great white shark occasionally blends considerable caution with aggression. Each time the shark rushed at him, says Dr. Nelson, he scared it off by shouting and at the same time threateningly wielding his speargun.

White sharks often trail ships for days on end. A sixteenth-century Portuguese traveler to India has recorded that one of these ship-followers found its perseverance well rewarded when a man fell overboard from the ship it had been following for days.

TIGER SHARK

If the white shark is the terror of the temperate seas, the tiger shark must be considered *the* man-eater of the tropical seas. There have been more human victims of the tiger shark than perhaps of any other species. In India, Indonesia, Japan, the Philippines, in South Africa, Australia and the Caribbean, the tiger shark is regarded as the most dangerous of all sharks. Not that it is more ferocious than other sharks: Indeed, it is less aggressive than the white and nearly as cautious as the blue shark. What makes it *the* man-eater among sharks is its greater presence inshore where it has easy access to swimmers, surfers, and other prospective human victims. In-donesians fear attacks from tiger sharks even in knee-deep water. Such attacks in American waters are not altogether unheard of. Dr.

Eugenie Clark has reported an attack by a five-foot tiger shark on a boy swimming ten feet from the shore in Florida.

Growing to a maximum size of thirty feet, the tiger shark can easily deal out death to swimmers and fishermen on its frequent incursions into inshore waters. In August 1967, a tiger shark attacked Robert Bartle of Perth, Australia, while he was spear-fishing. Suddenly, as if from nowhere, reports an eye-witness, the shark appeared and seized Bartle in its jaws and, biting his body in two just below the ribs, swallowed the lower half in one piece. Such a feat for a tiger shark is nothing unusual, considering that it is endowed with razor-sharp teeth, extremely powerful jaws, and an inordinately large mouth.

HAMMERHEAD SHARK

Another dangerous shark is the hammerhead. There are four or five different species of hammerhead sharks, but the great hammerhead is generally regarded as the most dangerous. It lives generally in warm seas, but in summer it is often sighted in temperate seas as well. It is a fish that moves freely between inshore and offshore waters, and so it can be dangerous to swimmers and surfers. The adult hammerhead shark ranges in size from ten feet to fifteen feet.

Hammerhead sharks eat almost all varieties of sea creatures, among them other sharks, not excluding members of the hammerhead family. Their taste for human flesh is displayed occasionally by attacks on humans in the Pacific, Atlantic and Indian oceans. They have attacked fishermen, skin-divers and swimmers, in Asian,

African, and South and Central American waters. They are also known to have attacked victims of boating accidents. One such victim was Robert Walter who, on September 26, 1959, was attacked by a hammerhead shark after his boat capsized in the Gulf of Mexico. Before he was rescued, the shark had so severely wounded and lacerated his body that he had to be given numerous stitches. Inshore attacks by hammerhead sharks are not unusual. A few years ago, a Florida woman was attacked while swimming one hundred and fifty yards from the shore. Hammerhead sharks have also reportedly attacked fishing boats and bitten holes in them.

Because of the peculiar shape of its head, this species is the most easily identified of all sharks. Opinions vary as to the biological function of its hammer-shaped head. It is generally agreed, however, that the head serves as a rudder and also as an aid in balancing. The functional utility of the shark's oddly placed eyes has been another matter for much puzzlement. In a full-grown hammerhead, the distance between the two eyes could be no less than two feet. Experts tend to regard the nerve cells spread over the shark's body as having a greater role in helping it "see" its environment than do its bizarre eyes.

The nightmarish aspect of this species has often been noted. The grotesque shape of its head and its jerky back-and-forth movement as the weird creature makes its way through the water, give it an eerie appearnace that is apt to fill the mind of the beholder with surrealistic fears. More than any other shark, the hammerhead could generate in man the kind of terror associated with the fabled monsters of myth and legend.

GREAT BLUE SHARK

Once considered harmless by several scientific authorities, the great blue shark is regarded as positively dangerous by those who have come in close contact with it — divers, swimmers, sailors and lifeguards. This is the most numerous of all large sharks in North American seas, indeed in all temperate waters. Ranging in size from ten to twelve feet, the great blue shark with its brilliant blue color and its slim, streamlined body, is perhaps the most beautiful of all sharks, a "graceful killer" that usually hunts in the open sea, coming inshore less frequently than the hammerhead. Because of its beauty, the religious imagination of the ancient Tahitians envisaged the blue shark as the shadow of Handsome Shark, consort of the sky goddess, Taarea. A nine-foot blue will weigh only about 175 pounds whereas a tiger shark of the same length will weigh not less than 700 pounds; but the blue shark is nonetheless dangerous.

There have been numerous reports of attacks on humans by blue sharks. In the last century, a small group of Mexican soldiers, attempting to cross from Santa Cruz Island to the mainland in a flimsy boat, were attacked and killed (all but one of them) by a pack of blue sharks. On November 10, 1959, Duffie Fryling, a lifeguard, was attacked by several blue sharks while he was swimming about seventy-five yards offshore. When the fishing boat *Spare Time* sank ten miles off Santa Monica on July 27, 1952, blue sharks attacked some of the survivors struggling in the water. On July 28, 1957, Earl Murray, a professional diver, was attacked by a six-foot blue shark, but he managed to escape unhurt by using the butt of his spear to keep the shark at bay. Not so lucky was Lieutenant J. C. Neal who, while scuba diving off Panama City, Florida, was killed by what is presumed to be a blue shark.

*The blue shark's danger to man is disputed,
but its habit of following ocean-going vessels and feeding
on discarded garbage gives it the opportunity to menace victims
of ship or plane wrecks. (U.S. Navy)*

An interesting account of an attack by a blue shark is that by Pete Peterson, who, as he admits, provoked the shark by teasing it with a bait which he dangled tantalizingly before its snout without letting it have it. Enraged, the shark rammed its body against the skiff with full force and made straight for a photographer who was shooting its performance from nearby. The photographer hit it on the snout with his camera and managed to clamber on to the skiff, just in time.

Ancient shark lore has credited the great blue shark with immense parental solicitude for the well-being of its young even to the extent of swallowing them in order to protect them from their enemies. The modern observer, however, will be inclined to be less edified than the ancients, and will, with good reason, "admire" the blue shark for its voracious appetite!

MAKO SHARK

Like the great blue shark, the mako is slim and beautiful. Because of its brilliant blue color and its great speed, it has been called "blue lightning." The adult mako ranges in size from eight to thirteen feet. Though its habitat is mainly tropical, it is found in temperate waters as well. In the American Pacific, mako sharks are seen as far north as central California, while in the Atlantic, they sometimes go as far up as Nova Scotia. The mako prefers the open sea to shallow or inshore waters, though it may occasionally venture inshore in search of small fish.

The mako is an aggressive fish: It shows none of the caution that characterizes the blue shark. Stories abound of attacks by makos on men and boats in the Caribbean, in the South Seas, and in the Pacific

The mako is one of the swiftest swimmers of the shark family and often leaps from the water in graceful, natural movement. (Marineland of Florida)

Ocean. These attacks have often been made by schools of makos, not by single individuals. One such attack took place in the sea off the Ellice Islands, in the western Pacific, north of the Fiji Islands, when one of several canoes carrying forty islanders was capsized by a squall. A school of makos that had been trailing the canoes lost no time in tearing to pieces the victims of the squall. They then butted and rammed the other canoes until they went to pieces or were over-turned. The sharks killed all but two of the forty islanders.

Of all the sharks, the mako is considered the best game fish. Sharks are generally considered poor game by most sportsmen. Once hooked, most sharks give up and sulk after a brief struggle. Not so the mako. It hits back at its attackers and their boats with astounding ferocity and vigor. Its great leaps into the air when hooked have thrilled many a sportsman who considers it worthwhile going through a lot of trouble to see this spectacular aerial feat. Zane Grey first discovered and extolled in his writings the thrills and excitements of mako fishing. Nobel-Prize-winning novelist Ernest Hemingway was another deep-sea angler who knew the excellence of the mako as a game fish. In 1936, he landed a 768-pound mako off Bimini in the Bahamas.

The attitude of most fishing "sportsmen" toward the shark is shockingly callous, utterly devoid of any feeling for the shark as a fellow-creature. One of them writes: "Men hate sharks and have hated them for centuries. History is full of stories about human beings being chewed to bits by these voracious beasts. Every sailor who has ever been shipwrecked has a worse dread of sharks than death itself. Commercial fishermen are particular enemies of sharks, which have killed and injured so many fishermen besides continually ripping up their nets. Men have begun now to hit back. Very gradually shark fishing is becoming a great sport and if this trend continues, thousands of fishermen all over the world will begin to take their toll of these killers."

These words are typical of the average sportsman's attitude toward sharks: They exemplify the obtuse conscience of those pathological seekers of excitement who call the animal a vicious predator when it kills for food and yet pride themselves on being "great" sportsmen when they kill for pleasure.

Most shark-hunting sportsmen go to sea to take it out on the shark for being a man-eater. In doing so they forget that not all sharks are man-eaters and that, if it were simply a matter of tit for tat, of blood for blood, the shark would have to kill thousands of men annually to get even with man. Attacks on men by sharks are totted up to add to the shark's ill-repute, while those by men on sharks are lauded as triumphs of angling or deep-sea fishing, or as feats of harpooning and "dragon" slaying.

The anti-shark crusader whose anathema against sharks was quoted above has the naiveté to execrate the shark for not being a good "sport" by obligingly offering itself to the gaff of its assailant. "A shark," says he, "is nasty even when he is on his best behavior, and he tries to hide under the boat to avoid the gaff—very unsporting conduct." One almost feels that the shark, if ever it heard this magisterial pronouncement against its species, would promptly reform its conduct, if only to redeem its reputation as a game fish!

Another "great" sportsman, who specializes exclusively in shark fishing, calls his sport "monster fishing," thus ascribing to himself the heroic role of the dragon killers of myth and legend. This man has the singular distinction of having killed more sharks than "anyone in history," and we may safely assume that, when the history of our times is written centuries from now, his name will be gratefully memorialized as the twentieth-century scourge of sharks!

The man-eaters discussed in this chapter are chiefly responsible for man's animus toward the shark. Among other sharks that are dangerous to man must be counted the whaler shark, the lemon shark, the dusky shark, and the whitetip shark. In labeling only a few sharks as man-eaters we do not imply that other sharks are unlikely to attack humans. In fact, all sharks are potentially dangerous, even the smallest ones. Since sharks can bite and have sharp teeth and powerful jaws, it would be imprudent for anyone not to be wary of them wherever they are encountered — in deep water or shallow, in the open sea, or in a river or lake, or even in an aquarium pool.

Plentiful along Florida coasts and in the Caribbean, lemon sharks feed in shallow coastal waters. Because they frequent inshore waters, lemon sharks are potentially dangerous to swimmers. (Marineland of Florida)

"A shark! A shark!" I rushed out of the writing room and was shown a black triangle sticking out of the water some fifty meters from the ship, and moving in our direction. It was the fin of the dread monster."

Albert Schweitzer, *The Animal World of Albert Schweitzer*

A good nibble or bite is my chiefest delight,
When I'm merely expected to see,
But a bite from a fish is not quite what I wish,
When I get it performed upon me.

Lewis Carroll, "The Two Brothers"

The Anatomy of the Consummate Killer

Prudence or wariness in approaching sharks or in entering the water where their presence may be expected will, no doubt, make for greater safety from them, but not all victims of shark attacks can be accused of having been imprudent or unwary. A girl bather whose arm was bitten off by a shark in just two and a half feet of water, and a young boy whose penis was snipped by a little shark that leaped up from less than knee-deep water were the victims of the fortuitous factor in the shark's unpredictable ways. Nor did airmen or seamen who were cast at sea and attacked by sharks deliberately court disaster.

On December 7, 1941, when a torpedoed British cruiser went down in the South Atlantic, sharks converged on the scene almost immediately and feasted on the survivors struggling in the water. Another tragedy of a similar nature, but far more disastrous in terms of human lives lost, occurred a year later when the troop ship *Nova Scotia* sank off the coast of South Africa, delivering about a thousand men to the sharks. The Caribbean Sea became the scene of another tragedy of this kind in 1969 when the survivors of an air disaster were killed by sharks.

Attacks on individuals by single sharks are far more numerous. These attacks have occurred inshore and offshore, in ocean depths and on the surface, in fresh water lakes and in rivers far inland. And the assailants have been sharks of all sizes from two-footers to the larger killers.

Several years ago when a steamer sank in the Zambesi River in Africa, seventeen of the passengers were killed by sharks. The Congo, too, has its share of dangerous sharks. Sharks in Lake Nicaragua take a substantial toll of human lives. The Tigris and the Euphrates as well as the Ganges and a few other rivers in India contain sharks that have taken hundreds of lives. Ganges sharks in the Hooghly river in Calcutta once proved so dangerous to bathers that rewards were given to those who caught them.

Among the most surprising, and not the least tragic, have been attacks on unsuspecting persons lingering in supposedly safe waters. A few years ago, a girl surfer at Manzanillo, Mexico, had a breast torn off by a shark, and in 1959 a woman was attacked by a four-foot shark in shallow water near Clearwater, Florida. A year earlier, a ten-year-old boy lost a leg to a five-foot shark in water just three feet deep at Sarasota, Florida.

Nowhere else are attacks in shallow water so frequent as in Australia. Several Australians, among them a Prime Minister, have lost their lives to sharks. Theo Brown believes that Harold Holt, the late Australian Prime Minister who allegedly drowned while swimming at Cheviot Beach, Portsea, Victoria, on December 17, 1967, must, from all evidence, have died of a shark attack.

Shark attacks, which have always attracted headlines, have attained greater news value recently on account of *Jaws*, the sensational shark movie that has induced something of a shark pyschosis in the public mind. Perhaps because of this there were more than the usual number of reported shark attacks in the months after the film was released. In July-August 1975, there were about twelve reports of attacks in American coastal waters and elsewhere. One of these attacks took place on August 12, 1975, when twenty-year-old Henry Peterson of Beloit, Wisconsin, was bitten on the right leg by a five-foot shark while he was swimming in waist-deep water at Daytona Beach, Florida. He was rescued, but his leg had to be amputated. The news story reporting this incident noted that four other assaults on humans had occurred earlier during the same season along an eighty-mile stretch of the U.S. Atlantic coast. Another incident reported during the same period involved twenty-three-year-old Robert Rebstock who was attacked by an eighteen-foot shark while he was diving for abalone off Point Conception, California. Having swallowed him up to the thigh, the shark dropped him for a second attack. Instantly, his companions managed to rescue him from the monster. Far more tragic was the fate of Bobby R. Slack, an American domiciled in Australia, who was swallowed whole by an enormous shark.

What is particularly remarkable about shark attacks is their devastating nature. People have been mauled, mangled, mutilated, bitten in half or swallowed whole. Up to eighty percent of shark attack victims die either immediately or later — from fatal wounds, from shock, from loss of blood.

What makes the shark such a consummate killer? In the first place, sharks have powerful jaws with a biting pressure of several tons per square inch. Secondly, most of them are endowed with sharp teeth that can cut through the toughest material. They have been rightly described as "living tooth factories," and as "nature's most 'all-out' experiment with teeth." Unlike the teeth of the bony fishes, shark's teeth are not "rooted" in sockets, but are affixed to the gums. For this reason, teeth are often lost by being lodged in the body of the shark's victim in the course of an attack. But, in most sharks, lost teeth are quickly replenished from the many rows of teeth behind the functional row in front. In fact, the shark can well afford to be blithely prodigal in the use of its teeth, since there is practically no limit to its capacity to replace lost or worn-out teeth.

Furthermore, the shark is unique among fishes in having teeth with serrated edges, though not all sharks are endowed with such teeth. Serrated teeth, which are useful in slashing huge chunks of meat off the big prey, are found only in the larger predators among sharks. These teeth are so efficient in cutting through flesh, bone, hide or shell that, by comparison, the teeth of the terrestrial predators such as the lion would seem "crude and inefficient." Such efficient teeth enable the large pelagic sharks to cut through the shell of a sea turtle, to bite holes in dories and canoes, to saw off a human leg at the thigh, or to cut a man in half all in an instant. These teeth are so sharp that primitive Pacific islanders have used them as shaving razors, and as weapons of war. In Polynesia, women once wore shark's teeth as ornaments, which also served as deterrents to would-be rapists.

In addition to its incredible teeth and powerful jaws, the shark's entire physiology is geared to making it the perfect predator. It has already been noted that sharks can attain greater speeds than many other fish that are supposed to be faster swimmers. Not having the swim-bladder indeed has the disadvantage of making it necessary for the shark to be constantly in motion, but it gives the shark an advantage over the bony fishes especially in swift up-and-down movements through the water. Whereas the speed with which the bony fishes ascend and descend is dependent on the expansion and contraction of the swim-bladder, the shark's speed in such movements is determined by its own energy, and it is free from the risk the bony fishes have of bursting their swim-bladder if their speed does not synchronize with the inflation and deflation of the bladder. The shark's speed and efficiency as a swimmer is a factor

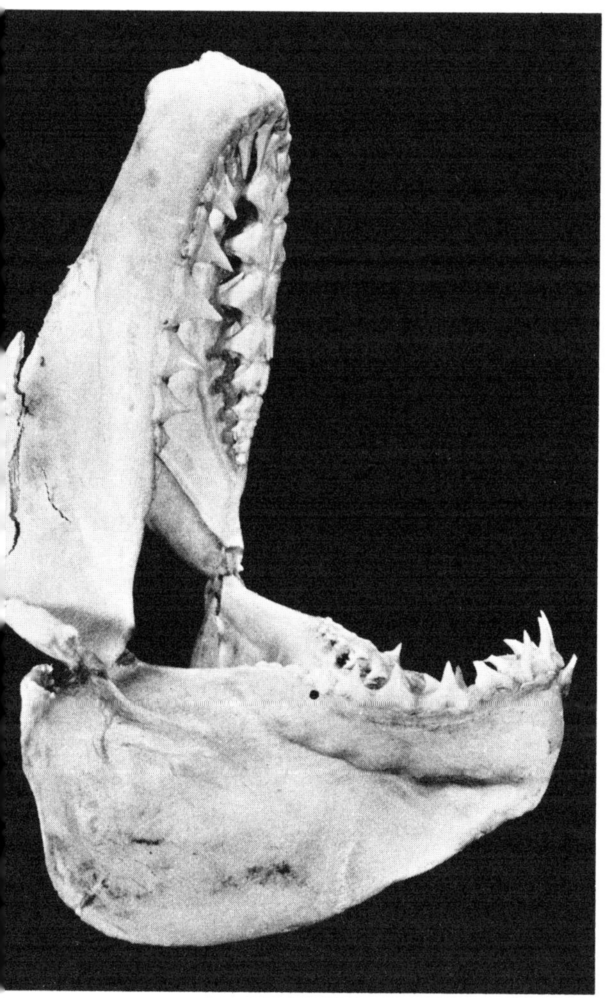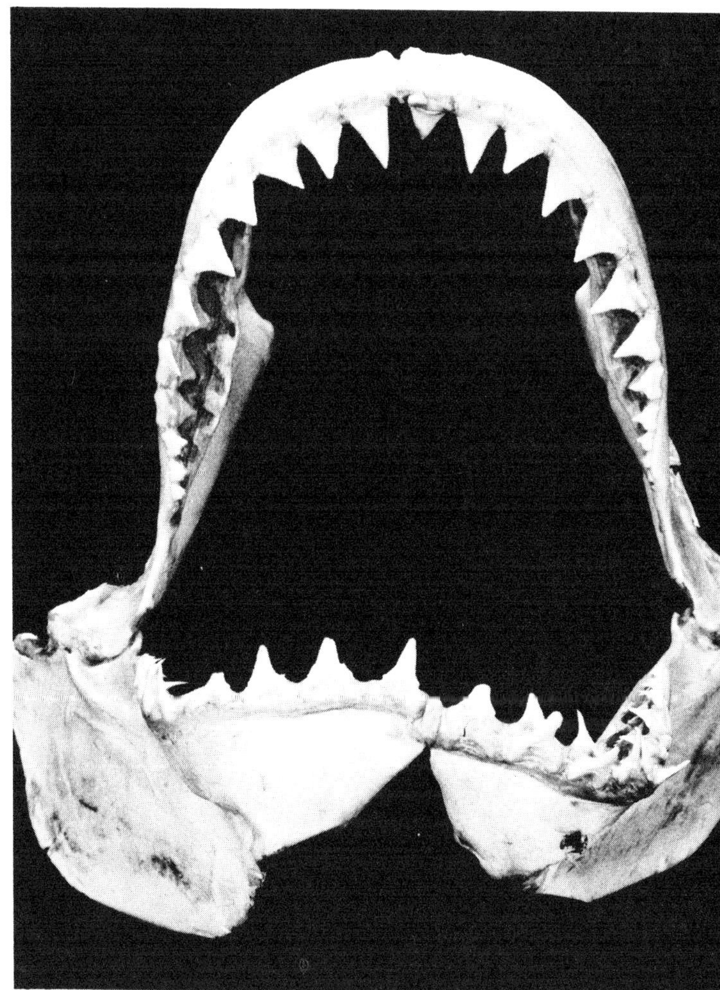

Profile (left) and frontal (right) views of the jaws of a great white shark expose the formidable teeth. Such powerful jaws are capable of removing ten pounds of flesh in a single bite. (Marineland of Florida)

that adds significantly to its efficiency as a predator. Some shark experts have credited the shark with greater speed than even the dolphin and the porpoise, which are generally regarded as the fastest swimmers in the ocean.

Speed and splendid teeth, however, would hardly have sufficed to give the shark its preeminence as a predator, if it were not for the faculties of perception that enable it to sense the presence of its prey from considerable distances within its territorial vicinity. These faculties are sight, smell, and "hearing."

Although folklore has traditionally attributed poor eyesight to the shark, modern experts are generally of the opinion that the shark's vision plays no negligible role in its search for food. It seems reasonable to assume that the shark, after millions of years of adapting to the aquatic world, must be able to see better in its natural habitat than the scuba diver or the oceanic explorer. Several experienced divers have expressed their conviction that the shark can see a diver in deep ocean from a distance at which the diver can hardly see the shark. According to Professor Perry W. Gilbert, the shark's eyes are capable of distinguishing forms and shapes from considerable distances, and can do so even in dim light. Bright objects that stand out in color from their surroundings attract the attention of the shark more easily than do others. Evidence of this is provided by what happened when a military aircraft ditched into the Pacific Ocean a few years ago. Those among the crew who wore orange-colored flying suits were attacked and killed by sharks, while those who wore green suits remained unhurt and were rescued.

While sight is important in the shark's hunt for food, the shark's sense of smell is of even greater importance in this regard. Sharks can smell blood and react to it from considerable distances — from a mile away, according to one aerial study. Laboratory studies have shown that the shark, deprived of the sense of smell, could swim past food without being aware of its presence. Some experts are of the opinion that in "choosing" a human victim from among a crowd of bathers, the shark might well be led by the peculiar odor of that person, or by the smell of blood from a wound.

More important than either smell or sight or both in detecting prey is the shark's sensitivity to vibrations caused by objects moving in the water. Like other fishes, shark's have what is called the lateral line, which consists of a series of canals running, below the skin, along either side of the shark's head and body. These canals, which contain mucus, are connected with the water through tiny pores in the skin, and are thus exposed to the vibrations in the water, including those produced by any fish in distress. These vibrations pass through the mucus and oscillate the tiny hairlike "feelers" reaching out from the sensory cells or neuromasts located inside the canals. The signals thus received by the neuromasts are transmitted to the brain through the nervous system, thereby giving the shark its first intimation of the presence of prey within its vicinity. Triggered by this message, the shark moves toward the source of the vibrations, and then smells its prey before seeing it. Even in the absence of smell or visibility, however, it can still reach its prey by means of its automatic gravitation toward the source from which the vibrations received in its brain have emanated.

The virtual autodynamism of the shark's hunting movements is an aspect of the shark that typifies the almost mechanical efficiency with which it responds to the presence of prey. Quite appropriately, it has been called a "killing machine," and it is part of the enigma of the shark's nature that it is at once "the most mechanical" of animals and the most unpredictable.

If the shark is a "killing machine," it is not, as Philippe Cousteau points out, "a killer without a cause." In being a predator and a killer, the shark is no more "guilty" than are the other inhabitants of both sea and land. In fact, there are many smaller creatures that are relatively more predatory than the shark. For instance, Konrad Z. Lorenz, the famous naturalist, has shown in his book *King Solomon's Ring*, how much more voracious and predatory, in its own small way, is the water shrew, the smallest of all mammals. Compared to the immense appetite of the water shrew and its capacity to eat the equivalent of its own weight or more of food daily, the food habits of the shark would seem abstemious! And yet the shrew, like the shark, is only acting inevitably in accord with the dictates of its own nature. As Theo Brown puts it, "the killing of one living thing by another form of life is the order of survival, with nothing being wasted in nature. Only man is the indiscriminate killer, slaughtering for material gain, for revenge, for lust, for pleasure."

Typical of man's lust for pleasure and his hatred of sharks is the behavior of a Californian "sportsman" mentioned by Webster. This man claimed that he hated sharks because of their predatory nature, but he "outsharked" the shark in predatoriness by killing more than two hundred of the species for sport. Of such people, who do not know the difference between sport and slaughter, Philippe Cousteau has aptly said that they "would be more at home in a psychiatric clinic than in their 'sporting clubs.'"

Sharks are infamous for their ravenous appetites and catholic diet.

William J. Crombie, *The Living World of the Sea*

Oh, 'twas in the broad Atlantic
'Mid the equinoctial gales
That a young fellow fell overboard
Among the sharks and whales . . . .

Writer of Song Unknown

The Omnivore

Unlike the human hunter, the shark hunts only for food. In its hunt for food, the shark is simply following instinct: It is instinct incarnate. From the very moment of its birth, the shark displays its instinctive gravitation toward food or anything it mistakes for food. Jacques Cousteau mentions the case of some baby sharks delivered by a Caesarean operation on a dying female tiger shark. They were thrown into the water straight from their mother's uterus. Immediately, one of them seized in its jaws a wooden stick that Cousteau was holding in his hand to drive away the sea urchins from where he was working in the water. The way it grabbed and violently shook the stick, says Cousteau, exactly duplicated the adult tiger shark's mode of attack on its prey.

In at least one species of shark — the sand tiger shark — the predatory instinct is active even during its prenatal life. The female sand tiger shark has two uteri. Eggs are hatched within both. The first baby shark hatched within each uterus feeds on the babies hatched subsequently. Steward Springer, the man who discovered this interesting phenomenon, was bitten on the hand by one of these prenatal predators while he was examining a pregnant shark.

The intrauterine cannibalism of the baby sand tiger shark has no known counterpart in the prenatal life of other sharks, but postnatal cannibalism is nothing unusual in the shark world. It is not uncommon, among many species, for the mother shark to eat its own young. We have already seen how the blue shark's habit of eating its young was misconstrued by the ancients to be a touching example of parental solicitude for the offspring's safety. Bodies of adult sharks have often been found in the stomachs of most of the pelagic species. Any wounded shark in a pack is invariably "finished off" by its fellows. Sharks have been found quite capable of devouring parts of their own bodies. Theo Brown once disemboweled a shark and threw it back into the sea. He then threw down its innards, which the shark immediately swallowed, only to have them come out through the slit in its stomach. Other wounded sharks are known to have curled round and snapped up their own entrails or other organs hanging loose from their gashed bodies.

Apart from these gastronomic extremes, the shark is a thorough omnivore, a true-blue gormandizer, with no reservations about eating almost any kind of food. The shark's diet is predominantly piscine: It includes quite a wide spectrum of the ocean's multitudinous life. Even a modest list of the sea creatures that constitute the shark's "cosmopolitan" menu forms a representative inventory of marine life, not excluding sea snakes or sea turtles, or even dolphins and porpoises, of which the shark is supposed to be afraid. While dissecting sharks, Theo Brown has found in their bellies the remains of creatures such as starfish, including the highly poisonous Crown of Thorns. There is a popular notion that sharks shun the striped sea snake because of its extreme poisonousness. Pennsylvania State University biologist William Dunson has set himself the task of verifying the truth of this belief. Serving as chief scientist aboard the ship, *Alpha Helix*, belonging to the Scripps Institution of Oceanography, Dunson proposes to conduct research in the Visayan Sea off the Philippines where striped sea snakes are numerous. By catching and dissecting sharks in these waters to see if their stomachs contain any striped sea snakes, Dunson hopes to establish beyond doubt whether or not, as commonly believed, sharks give a wide berth to these snakes.

Sharks, however, are known to have eaten other poisonous sea creatures with impunity. Theo Brown claims that "none of the venomous or poisonous marine animals appears to dampen the appetite of a shark, for while examining one specimen I found two poisonous barbs from a stingray firmly embedded in its stomach wall. The shark appeared healthy, with a large and well-developed liver, always an accurate indication of their condition."

If the shark's metabolic capacity to nullify the deleterious effects of the virulent biotoxins ingested along with its outlandish diet is a matter for wonderment, no less marvelous is its ability to swallow huge sea turtles, large clams and other hard-shelled creatures without rupturing the walls of its stomach or overtaxing the digestive powers of its intestines. Other marine animals that may be found inside sharks include: seals, crayfish, sea urchins, octopuses. Among non-marine animals that have been found in sharks are: cats, birds, alligators, crocodiles. A giant shark caught in Australian waters had an entire horse in its belly!

The reckless inclusiveness of the shark's dietary audacity is such that, quite often, the contents of its stomach have been found to include an incredible assortment of inedible objects that could work havoc in less sturdy stomachs. The "alien" objects that have found their way in through the capacious jaws of these marine Gargantuas include: bottles, boots, plastic floats, rope, rocks, beer cans, sacks, telephone books, cork, sail canvas, cardboard, ship's papers, pots and pans, pieces of metal, a wooden butter box, a keg of nails, a huge roll of roofing paper, the propeller of an outboard motor.

In at least one case, objects found in the stomach of a shark have had fateful consequences on the lives of men. The men in this case were the captain and crew of an eighteenth-century American brig engaged in privateering operations against British ships in the Caribbean Sea. Apprehended by a British man-of-war, the captain threw the ship's papers into the sea. He and his crew were, however, taken to Port Royal, Jamaica, for trial. They were about to be set free for want of proper evidence when another British ship arrived in port with the needed documents recovered from a shark that had swallowed the captain's papers. On the irrefutable evidence provided by these papers, the captain and his crew were condemned. Known as the "Shark Papers," these documents are still preserved in a museum in Jamaica.

Of course, it would be worthwhile to learn the secret of the shark's ability to swallow such atrocious oddities of non-food without jeopardizing its health. The quest for this secret could be all the more intriguing, if not rewarding, in view of the fact that, despite its scandalous eating habits, the shark is noted for its resistance to cancer, heart diseases, and other ailments common to human beings. At any rate, the shark's digestive system is eminently suited to accommodate the vagaries of its unpredictable menu. The shark has extremely short intestines. As compared with an adult human's thirty-foot-long intestines, a nine-foot shark's intestines will be no more than seven feet in length. If, for this reason, the shark's food is exposed to less digestive surface, the digestive process itself is considerably prolonged by the cork-screw-shaped valve that slows down the food's passage through the intestines. The shortness of the shark's intestines is more than compensated for by the unique digestive devices built into them.

It must be noted, however, that the shark is not totally immune from the hazards of its indiscriminate eating. The porcupine fish, for instance, can do more harm to the shark than he bargains for when he nonchalantly snaps it up on his hunt for bigger prey. Caught in the mouth of the shark, the victim inflates itself immediately, thus blocking the passage of water through the shark's gills, and thereby asphyxiating him. The Pacific Island inhabitants employ an ingenious method of catching sharks by taking advantage of the shark's propensity to swallow almost anything. After attracting a large pack of sharks by strewing the water with bits of fish, they throw into the water several boiled jam melons. The outside shell of these melons cools off immediately, while their inner contents retain the heat. The unsuspecting sharks promptly devour the melons, only to float up to the surface later from the fatal effect of their heated contents.

An aspect of the shark that calls for comment but eludes explanation is its ability to retain substantial portions of its stomach's contents undigested for long periods. A fifteen-foot tiger shark captured in Australian waters and kept in a zoo tank for three weeks before it died was found to have in its stomach two well-preserved dolphins it had devoured some time before it was caught. Another Australian shark episode provides further proof of the shark's ability to keep items of food intact in its stomach. Some years ago, a young woman lost her left arm to a shark. When the shark was captured eight days later, the arm was found well-preserved in its belly. A ring the woman was wearing at the time she lost her arm was still on one of the fingers. The woman thereafter wore the ring on her right hand. The shark's unique capacity to retain its prey within its stomach for prolonged periods seems to lend substance to the contention (noted in the prologue) of the eighteenth-century Swedish naturalist, Carolus Linnaeus, that the Biblical "fish" that held Jonah in its belly for three days must, in fact, have been a shark.

Another matter for surprise and speculation has been the fact that, despite its inclusive dietary habits, the shark appears to have a discriminating taste in regard to human flesh. Folklore was far ahead of science in attributing to the shark a certain degree of choosiness in the matter. Native divers in the Red Sea, for instance, were allegedly safe from the sharks swimming around, while any white person who ventured into the water would be immediately gobbled up. The natives believed that they were spared because of their votive gestures to the spirits incarnate in the sharks. On the other hand, among white people in the New World, it was believed that sharks had a special preference for blacks. Slave-owning whites, when they went swimming, used to have themselves ringed by a number of black swimmers, in the hope that any man-eating shark that came by would spare them in preference for the blacks.

Another popular notion about the shark's preferences in regard to human flesh — one that has, of late, found advocates in the scientific world — is that sharks prefer men to women. Scott Johnson, a biophysicist at the Naval Undersea Center in San Diego, California, said recently that a study of recorded shark attacks had revealed that sharks "prefer men better than nine to one." Whatever be the reason for this alleged preference (which Johnson describes as inexplicable), there are, as with other aspects of shark behavior, exceptions which must be taken into account. There is, for instance, the case of a shark that passed by the men in a crowded Australian beach and loitered about a spot nearby where only women bathed.

Whatever be the truth of the matter, the shark's approach to man, whether as prospective prey or enemy, is generally one of caution. Caution, in fact, is characteristic of the shark's approach to all big prey, and it has been the shark's surest guarantee for survival through the ages. When the presence of prey is registered in its brain through the lateral line, as has been noted, the shark swims toward its prey, which may initially be out of sight. When it comes within sight of the prey, the shark starts going round it cautiously. Gradually, the circling narrows until the shark bumps the prey with its snout. This is regarded as the shark's way of tasting its meal before eating it. If the taste is good, the shark soon takes a bite, which will be followed by a relentless series of attacks. This pattern is followed only when a lone shark, or just two or three sharks, confront would-be prey. When there is a whole pack of sharks, the circling ceremony might be altogether eliminated in the frenzied rush of a collective onslaught. No human, or any other creature for that matter, will survive such an attack.

Man is not the only mammal that occasionally becomes the shark's prey. Marine mammals such as dolphins, porpoises and wounded or dead whales are sometimes added to the shark's diet. The shark often follows herds of these mammals in the hope of feeding on stray weaklings or sick and dying members. Both sharks and dolphins are wary of each other and normally avoid head-on encounters. If the shark's jaws and teeth give it a definite advantage over the dolphin, the latter's superior intelligence enables it to hold its own against the shark. In fact, the ability of dolphins to organize collective attacks on the shark is a factor that considerably mitigates its invincibility as the most naturally endowed predator of the seas.

But the shark's most formidable enemy is a non-marine mammal, man: Man, that is, armed with a spear, a speargun, a harpoon, a gaff, or any of the deadly weapons that can completely negate the shark's physical superiority as a killer in terms of size, strength, jaw power, and dental armament. And it is ultimately in its encounter with man that the shark's incredibly long tenure on earth is likely to be threatened, if not endangered; for the enemy that the shark confronts in man is the only creature that has the capability to exterminate it if he chooses to do so. This temptation is likely to pose a serious problem as man, in the years to come, moves more and more into the shark's marine domain.

Sharp teeth, a pointed snout and dorsal fins of nearly
equal size are distinguishing characteristics of the sand shark.
(Marineland of Florida)

"You see," he went on after a pause, "it's as well to be provided for everything. That's the reason the horse has anklets around his feet."

"But what are they for?" Alice asked in a tone of great curiosity.

"To guard against the bite of sharks," the Knight replied. "It's an invention of mine."

Lewis Carroll, *Through the Looking Glass*

The island eats shark meat at noon

Gary Snyder, "Shark Meat"

. . . until everything
was rainbow, rainbow, rainbow!
And I let the fish go.

Elizabeth Bishop, "The Fish"

Sharks and Men

Will man use his power to exterminate the shark when he attempts to colonize the ocean? The answer is important. But a more immediate problem is how to save humans from sharks. Solving this problem should help prevent the extermination of sharks.

Most divers believe, from their own experience, that sharks are less likely to attack a diver than a swimmer. This is because a swimmer thrashing about on the surface produces signals similar to the convulsive movements of a dying fish, and these movements, signifying to the shark the presence of easy prey, are the very signals that trigger the shark's hunting instinct. The most likely moments when a diver may be attacked are when he is entering the water and when he is leaving it — at which times his movements resemble those of a fish in distress. The reason why sharks frequent popular beaches is that they are drawn by the "attractive" sounds produced by the bathers.

The most effective method devised so far to protect bathers on the beaches is meshing. This is a method by which sharks are trapped in gill nets placed near the beach. It has been used very successfully in both Australia and South Africa. In Australia where meshing has been used since 1937, only two attacks have so far occurred in meshed areas. Another method that has recently been given much consideration and seems to offer much hope is that of using trained dolphins to ward off sharks from beaches.

Some of the most gruesome shark events have been isolated attacks on individuals. Confronted by a shark, a swimmer or diver must avoid doing anything likely to activate its rapacity. He should not show fear, for, according to Jacques Cousteau, the shark is encouraged to attack when it recognizes fear — which it does instinctively. Any attempt to flee in an agitated manner will be tantamount to "inviting" an attack. The swimmer must, therefore, swim in a relaxed manner, using breast strokes rather than the splashy butterfly strokes, and he must take the utmost care not to lift his arms and legs above the water. The diver, likewise, must proceed at an even pace, keeping an eye on the shark lest it should attack him unawares. Nothing should be done that is likely to frighten the shark and provoke it to attack in self-defense. Neither should the swimmer or the diver remain motionless in the manner of a dead fish, thus making himself appear to the shark as easy quarry.

That courage, coolness and prudent behavior can mean all the difference between life and death to an unarmed swimmer in the presence of dangerous sharks has been proved on several occasions. In his autobiography, *An American Doctor's Odyssey*, Dr. Victor Heiser has described a classic experience of this kind. During a brief sojurn in a small town on the west coast of South America, he decided to have a swim, and dived from the local pier, not knowing that the sea in that area was shark-infested. When he had swum about a hundred yards, he suddenly found himself in the presence of a pack of about half a dozen hefty sharks. Frightened though he was and acutely aware of the danger he was in, Dr. Heiser decided that the only way to save himself was to keep his cool and swim back in just the same way as he had swum out from the pier. Accordingly, he calmly turned around and made his way back toward the pier with strong, steady, even strokes as a crowd of alarmed local people, who had earlier shouted in vain to warn him of the danger, watched anxiously from the pier. With the sharks trailing him dangerously close, but never attacking him, he managed at last to reach the safety of the pier amidst the cheers of the watching crowd.

Some of the methods traditionally believed to be effective in scaring sharks away have been found mostly ineffective. For instance, slapping the water or blowing bubbles may scare away small sharks, but no large shark can be expected to be thus intimidated. Slapping the water could indeed have the opposite effect: of attracting more sharks or inducing those at hand to attack.

Shouting is another method recommended to those in peril from aggressive sharks. This method may not be always effective, but it has driven off sharks in several instances. In 1943, when a German submarine was sunk off French West Africa, three of the survivors saved themselves from attacking sharks by putting their heads under water and shouting at them. Austrian diver Dr. Hans Hass who, with two other divers, dived in the Caribbean over a three-month period, has described in his book, *Diving to Adventure*, how he and his diving companions found shouting an effective way of scaring away sharks. He recounts this story:

> Sharks went for us like meteors and one of the three of us gave a cry of fear. None of us could remember afterwards who had cried out, but luckily it was a piercing shriek which went through the water with incredible results. At the last moment, as if stopped by some terrible blow, the three sharks wheeled away from us and bolted as fast as they had come. But one of the sharks . . . seemed after the first moment to be ashamed of its fear, for when it was about a hundred feet away, it turned back and threw itself furiously at us to begin a new attack. But this time we all shrieked in a chorus which had the effect, literally, of turning it over on its side and, seized with panic, it fled, never to return.

It must be noted, however, that shouting may not always prove as effective as in the cases mentioned above, especially when the danger is posed by one of the giant predators. Results obtained from studies made in the Red Sea by the Italian National Underwater Expedition led to the conclusion that underwater shouting is far from being universally effective.

Thanks to the many devices that have been invented to protect people from shark attacks, swimmers, divers and victims of air and sea disasters are not utterly defenseless against sharks. One of the most effective safety devices now available to oceanic researchers and victims of shipwreck is the "shark screen" which, when inflated, becomes a waterproof and scent-proof enclosure that isolates its occupant from any sharks around. Having tried this device and found it useful, Philippe Cousteau believes that it has "a good future."

Most of the protective devices currently in use are defensive weapons capable of seriously hurting or killing aggressive sharks. The best-known among them are the shark dart, the hypodermic spear, the bang-stick, the electric dart. Unlike these, the "shark billy," used by the Cousteaus and their diving companions, is a simple three-foot-long rod of wood with "non-slip points at one end." It enables the diver to keep the shark at bay without hurting or provoking it into a defensive attack.

Another method invented for protection against sharks is the use of shark repellents most of which depend on the shark's sense of smell or taste for their effectiveness. These chemical repellents, including the well-known "shark chaser," have generally been found useless. However, another form of repellent — the sonic repellent — holds out the promise of what appears to be perhaps the most satisfactory solution to the shark problem.

One of the first persons to indicate the possibility of using sound as a shark repellent was George Llano, author of *Airmen Against the Sea*. He based his theory on the experience of a pilot in the Pacific Ocean whose raft became the target of a pack of aggressive sharks that charged at it with extreme fury. Rubbing his fingers on the inside of the raft in helpless terror and desperation, the pilot was surprised to see the charging animals veer off at the last moment, obviously frightened by the squeaking sound produced by his involuntary act. From the experience of the pilot, Llano drew the conclusion that it should be possible to develop an effective shark repellent in the form of a mechanical device capable of producing frequencies of sound such as those produced by the pilot.

It was left to Theo Brown, however, to undertake serious research on an effective sonic repellent. Arriving independently at the same conclusion as did Llano, Brown set himself the task of discovering frequencies of sound capable of repelling all species of man-eating sharks anywhere in the ocean. He based his research on the principle that, because of the important role played by sharks in maintaining the ocean's ecological balance, "we must find ways and means of keeping the man-eating sharks at bay, rather than aiming at the wholesale and indiscriminate slaughter of the species."

Realizing that any repellent, to be effective, must aim at repelling the shark before its hunting instinct is activated, Brown ruled out the possibility of an effective repellent aimed at the shark's senses of smell and sight which register the presence of prey only after the brain has been "intimated" through the lateral line. Since the shark's attack pattern begins with the reception of vibrations in the brain, the sonic deterrent can be eminently effective in preventing the attack pattern from being set in motion.

To begin with, by using a transducer (underwater loudspeaker) located on the ocean floor to transmit "attractive" sounds identical to those that draw the shark to a dying or wounded fish, Brown was able to attract sharks to set targets. It was obvious, in these experiments, that neither smell nor sight had anything to do with the sharks' movement toward the target.

One of the most impressive results of Brown's experiments has been the discovery that attractive signals can be used to draw and excite large numbers of sharks into frenzied states of cannibalistic orgy. This may seem cruel, but there is nothing sadistic about Brown's ultimate goal, which is to find the right frequencies of sound that will drive sharks away instead of killing them. In fact, Brown is insistent that "the repellent signal used should merely repel, and not kill or injure the animals."

Further underwater experiments showed that, while the same signals are effective in attracting all sharks, different signals are needed to repel different species. This complicates the search, but Brown has already succeeded in finding the signals that repel three of the man-eating species — the whaler, the tiger, and the hammerhead — and he believes that it should be possible to discover the frequencies that repel the other man-eaters as well.

Once the frequencies capable of repelling all the dangerous species have been found, it should be technically possible, Brown believes, to cordon off beaches and harbors by means of sonic barriers. Divers, oceanic explorers, and survivors of air and sea disasters will be protected by small transmitting units. A major merit of the system envisaged by Brown is that, when perfected, it will be able to provide permanent protective barriers to future human settlements in the ocean. The sonic barrier will thus obviate the need to slaughter sharks wholesale.

Of all the experiments that have so far been made toward discovering an effective shark repellent, those conducted by Brown appear to be the most promising and the most satisfactory from the ecological viewpoint. Brown's approach to the shark is admirably responsive to the need for a more considerate and responsible attitude on man's part to his non-human fellow-creatures. It is remarkable that Brown, whose dedication to shark research was prompted by a young friend's death caused by a shark attack, can yet speak about sharks with great sympathy and understanding:

> It is often argued that sharks are cruel and vicious killers, unmercifully slaughtering every living thing they encounter. This I cannot accept, even after being involved in a number of attacks, including the fatal mauling of young Ken. I don't hate sharks. I have no emotional attitude towards them. I respect them as perhaps the most perfectly adapted killers on this planet; but otherwise I see them as simply marine animals, a primitive form of life obeying basic instinctive patterns, killing humans as they kill fish — for food. I don't fear them, but I do respect them as the most powerful creatures known to man, totally unpredictable, and to be treated with extreme caution and watched as you'd watch a savage dog. The more I work with sharks and try to increase my knowledge of their behavior, the less I seem to know. Although we have been successful in establishing general patterns of behavior, there is always the exception to the rule, the one shark that will completely reverse the expected trend. Sharks are no crueler than any other predator in the sea.

Brown's admission that the more he tries to increase his knowledge of sharks, the less he seems to know about them typifies the verdict of almost all shark researchers in assessing their knowledge of the shark after years of patient study. After more than thirty-three years of firsthand acquaintance with sharks, Jacques Cousteau, too, has felt obliged to admit that "the closer we come to sharks, the less we know of them." William J. Cromie, referring to the contradictions that abound in man's present-day knowledge of sharks and their ways, says:

> In fear and ignorance, man has cloaked them in mystery and misinformation. At one and the same time, they are portrayed as fearless killers and bullying cowards, as aggressive predators and dull-witted, self-propelled garbage cans.

What are sharks really like? No one can give an accurate answer. Zoologists who have devoted lifetimes to studying them cannot even generalize about their behavior or personality. After thousands of observations and hundreds of attacks on humans, man is not yet sure why they attack people and under what conditions.

In fact, the shark is the least understood of the earth's larger creatures and, for that reason, the least sympathized with. As Ken Schoenrock puts it, "The large cats were endangered and now they are protected. People understand them and want them to be protected. The wolf, formerly considered an enemy, is a good guy now. And this is only right: wolves are good guys. But the poor lonely shark is not understood. So little is known about the animal." What Farley Mowat (in *Never Cry Wolf*) has done for the wolf, Jane van Lawick-Goodall (in *My Friends, the Wild Chimpanzees*) for the chimpanzee, John MacKinnon (*In Search of the Red Ape*) for the orang-utan, and George Schaller (in *The Year of the Gorilla*) for the gorilla, no one has yet done for the shark.

And yet, it is imperative that man learn more about the shark — and with sympathy and understanding. Never before has he needed to know the shark and its ways as he does now. The seabed settlements of man's futuristic vision will not materialize unless man learns to ensure his safety from aggressive sharks without destroying them wholesale. The sonic barrier, which Theo Brown envisages as the final goal of his dedicated search, promises to be of immense value in the dual context of man's impending colonization of the ocean and of the new ecological enlightenment that calls for the least possible disruption of nature's equilibrium in the process. When the full range of "repelling" frequencies that Brown is looking for is found and when the mechanics of employing these frequencies as sonic barriers are perfected, man will have learned to prevent sharks from being dangerous to him. Thus man's intelligence will have found a way of establishing the basis for prolonged periods of coexistence between himself and the shark in the marine world.

Epilogue

This book, the reader need hardly be told now, was not meant to be just another scientific book about sharks. We have, to be sure, discussed, among other things, the biological aspects of sharks, but we have not made a fetish of "objectivity" and viewed these our fellow-denizens of planet Earth with the cold detachment of the scientist that chills "the genial current of the soul." We have tried to view sharks not simply as "jaws," but with sympathy and understanding.

Neither have we given much space to the names, shapes, colors and other peculiarities of many species of sharks which intrigue our curiosity, such as, for instance: the goblin shark whose name brings a touch of fantasy to the real world of fishes; the epaulette shark whose non-militant behavior belies its name and its looks; the Iago shark whose "honest" ways hardly evoke, in villainy or inhumanity, its notorious namesake in Shakespeare's *Othello*; the cigar shark which can offer nought but its lyric incandescence to the devotees of the fragrant weed; the zebra shark whose brilliant stripes are more than an eloquent apology for the absence of zebras in the marine world; the angel shark with its patterned symmetry that corporeally resembles the imagined form of its celestial model; the draughts-board shark that barks like a dog when pulled out of the water; the swell shark that, when caught, inflates itself, in the manner of a human egoist, to bluff its enemy by feigning bigness. And we have only glimpsed at the role of the shark in the marine ecology, at the unique aspects of its physiology, at the modes of reproduction whereby the different species of shark bring to fulfillment the promise of life's primordial behest: Increase and multiply.

We have, however, recognized that these "children" of the sea, be they the relatively small dogfish or huge leviathans such as the whale shark, be they the man-eating white sharks or the harmless basking sharks, are sharers with us in the élan vital of our planet. Konrad Lorenz's studies of animals and birds (*King Solomon's Ring, Studies in Animal and Human Behavior*) have demonstrated how much science can gain in true understanding by allowing the heart to play its rightful role in scientific investigation. He has shown what rewarding ties of trust, friendship and even "kinship" can be established between animal and man and what rare insights may be gained into both human and animal nature by the naturalist who brings a sympathetic disposition to the birds and beasts he studies. It is evident that with this kind of approach, a flower, for instance, can at once be a lesson in botany, anthropology and theology.

What this means in the present context is that any study of the shark, to be meaningful, must face the question: How does man relate to the shark? From a utilitarian or practical point of view, it is easy enough to consider the brute creation as part of the existential "other" that man must subdue and bring within his power, but, seen with the "eye of our immortal seeing," they are a part no less of the kingdom of life than of the kingdom within. It is only in the light of a higher ethic of compassion embracing all life that we will be able to understand the sublime insight of Albert Schweitzer who, as a boy, used to pray: "Dear God, guard and bless everything that breathes."

There are, of course, those who might say: All this is fine, but nature is cruel, and the shark itself is cruel. What can man do about it but be likewise? In answer to this, we shall say, with Konrad Lorenz, that "man should abstain from judging his innocently cruel fellow creatures," or, with Brigid Brophy, that "the whole case for behaving decently to animals rests on the fact that we are the superior species," — which is another way of saying that man, being man, must be more than just another predator, that he must be a preserver and protector of other species as well as his.

Appendix

Common name	Scientific name	Max length measured: U.S. coasts
Angel shark	*Squatina dumeril*	4 ft. 5 in.
Basking shark	*Cetorhinus maximus*	32 ft. 2 in.
Blue shark	*Prionace glauca*	11 ft.
Bonnethead	*Sphyrna tiburo*	3 ft. 7 in.
Bull shark	*Carcharhinus leucas*	9 ft. 10 in.
Chain dogfish	*Scyliorhinus retifer*	1 ft. 5 in.
Dusky shark	*Carcharhinus obscurus*	11 ft. 11 in.
Great hammerhead	*Sphyrna mokarran*	18 ft. 4 in.
Great white shark	*Carcharodon carcharias*	18 ft. 2 in.
Green dogfish	*Etmopterus virens*	0 ft. 11 in.
Greenland shark	*Somniosus microcephalus*	16 ft. 6 in.
Leopard shark	*Triakis semifasciata*	5 ft.
Mako shark	*Isurus oxyrinchus*	10 ft. 6 in.
Midwater dogfish	*Squaliolus sp.*	0 ft. 7 in.
Nurse shark	*Ginglymostoma cirratum*	9 ft. 3 in.
Porbeagle	*Lamna nasus*	10 ft.
Salmon shark	*Lamna ditropis*	8 ft. 6 in.
Sandbar shark	*Carcharhinus milberti*	7 ft. 8 in.
Sand shark	*Carcharias taurus*	10 ft. 5 in.
Saw shark	*Pristiophorus schroederi*	2 ft. 10 in.
Six-gilled shark	*Hexanchus sp.*	15 ft. 5 in.
Smooth dogfish	*Mustelus canis*	4 ft. 9 in.
Soupfin shark	*Galeorhinus zyopterus*	6 ft. 5 in.
Spiny dogfish	*Squalus acanthias*	5 ft. 3 in.
Thresher shark	*Alopias vulpinus*	18 ft.
Tiger shark	*Galeocerdo cuvieri*	13 ft. 10 in.
Whale shark	*Rhincodon typus*	38 ft.
Whitetip shark	*Carcharhinus longimanus*	11 ft. 6 in.

Max. length recorded: world	Traditional max. size from literature	Where Found
- - -	- - -	Northeastern Atlantic and Mediterranean
45 ft.	40-50 ft.	Temperate to northern seas
12 ft. 7 in.	25 ft.	Worldwide in tropical and temperate seas
- - -	6 ft.	Warm temperate zone of all oceans
- - -	10 ft.	Worldwide, been found in fresh-water lakes in Nicaragua, Guatemala and New Guinea
- - -	2 ft. 6 in.	Coastal waters of tropical and temperate regions in all oceans
- - -	15 ft.	Tropical and warm temperate waters on both sides of the Atlantic
- - -	15 ft.	Warm temperate zone of all oceans including Mediterranean Sea, both offshore and inshore
21 ft.	36 ft. 6 in.	Oceanic; tropical, subtropical, warm temperate belts especially in Australian waters
- - -	- - -	
21 ft.	24 ft.	Arctic seas
- - -	5 ft.	Pacific Ocean — Oregon to Baja California
12 ft.	12-13 ft.	Oceanic, tropical and warm temperate belts
- - -	- - -	
- - -	14 ft.	Caribbean and southeastern U.S. coast
12 ft.	12 ft.	Continental waters of northern Atlantic. Allied form in north Pacific, Australia and New Zealand
8 ft. 6 in.	12 ft.	Pacific Ocean
- - -	8 ft.	Tropical and temperate Atlantic Ocean
12 ft. 3 in.	15 ft. 11 in.	Indo-Pacific, Mediterranean, tropical West Africa, Gulf of Maine to Florida, Brazil, Argentina
- - -	- - -	South Africa and area from Australia to Korea
- - -	26 ft. 5 in.	Atlantic and Indian Oceans, South Africa and Mediterranean
- - -	5 ft.	Atlantic, Indian and Pacific oceans
6 ft. 5 in.	6 ft. 5 in.	
- - -	5 ft.	Northern Atlantic, northwestern Africa and Mediterranean
18 ft.	20 ft.	Most temperate and tropical seas
18 ft.	30 ft.	Tropical and subtropical belts of all oceans, inshore and offshore
45 ft.	45-50 ft.	All tropical oceans; reported as far north as Long Island
- - -	12 ft.	Pacific Ocean, offshore

Bull sharks are known to inhabit freshwater lakes and rivers
as well as the open seas. Here a bull shark plays host to a remora
that is attached securely to its underside. (Marineland of Florida)